Thursdays and Every Other Sunday Off

Thursdays and Every Other Sunday Off

A Domestic Rap by Verta Mae

Vertamae Smart-Grosvenor

Foreword by Premilla Nadasen

University of Minnesota Press
Minneapolis
London

Published by the University of Minnesota Press
111 Third Avenue South, Suite 290
Minneapolis, MN 55401-2520
http://www.upress.umn.edu

Printed in the United States of America on acid-free paper

The University of Minnesota is an equal-opportunity employer.

25 24 23 22 21 20 19 18   10 9 8 7 6 5 4 3 2 1

Library of Congress Cataloging-in-Publication Data
Names: Smart-Grosvenor, Vertamae, author.
Title: Thursdays and every other Sunday off : a domestic rap by Verta Mae / Vertamae Smart-Grosvenor.
Description: Minneapolis : University of Minnesota Press, 2018 | First edition published by Doubleday & Company, Inc., copyright 1972. | Includes bibliographical references.
Identifiers: LCCN 2018022269 | ISBN 978-1-5179-0607-8 (pb)
Subjects: LCSH: Household employees—United States. | African Americans—Social conditions.
Classification: LCC HD8039.D52 U85 2018 | DDC 331.4/816408996073—dc23
LC record available at https://lccn.loc.gov/2018022269

This book is dedicated to Ronald L. Hobbs and Lee Otis Johnson and it's for my daughters Chandra and Kali whom I pray will never have to work in Ms. Anne's kitchen and it's with sincere appreciation and much thanks to everyone who gave me their time and their stories and in memory of Clarice Ritter Williams, Mark Fisher, Albert Ayler, Betty Rawls, Clarence Funnye, Zell Ingram, Sonny Liston, Tami Terrel, Ray Richardson, Ralph Featherstone, Vashti Lowns, Jimi James Hendrix, William junebug White, Allie boy Bowser, Eva Hesse, Kathy Freyre, Hank Dammond, Lee Mogan, and Afalobi Adjai.

I wish to God every head of a family in the
United States had one slave to take the drudgery
and menial service off his family.

> —a prayer offered for the
> common man by
> President Andrew Johnson

Contents

Foreword

Premilla Nadasen

Vertamae Smart-Grosvenor was the ultimate storyteller. Her gift of storytelling is reflected in *Thursdays and Every Other Sunday Off: A Domestic Rap by Verta Mae*. The snippets, anecdotes, quotations, newspaper accounts, and historical references in this book are pieced together to form a mosaic that offers a compelling image of servitude in the African American experience and brings to light the travails and aspirations of Black workers. As a text, *Thursdays and Every Other Sunday Off* defies easy categorization. It is at once sociology, anthropology, history, poetry, and memoir. In an era when interdisciplinarity is understood as an essential methodological approach for a critical intellectual perspective, this book can be seen as a model of an interdisciplinary reading. The multiple sources on which Smart-Grosvenor draws, from Langston Hughes poems to history texts to magazine articles to her own recollections, create the possibility for a multilayered and deeply engaging analysis of domestic service.

Thursdays and Every Other Sunday Off is a collective account. By inviting people to contribute to her "domestic rap," Smart-Grosvenor crafted this book as a communal reflection of Black servitude. The conversations that comprise this book are a snapshot in time. The post–World War II period witnessed mass mobilizations among African Americans and opened up opportunities for a redefined racial order, which would ultimately overturn state support for legalized segregation. *Thursdays and Every Other Sunday Off* reflects the transformation of racial politics in the context of the Black freedom movement, of which a national struggle for domestic workers' rights was a critical part. It makes a case for the historical importance of domestic work as a core feature of racial oppression. But it also reflects a New Day. The anger, impatience, and fed-up-ness of the servant class palpably surface in the anecdotes Smart-Grosvenor shares. This book is both an alternate reading of Black history and a reclamation of dignity.

The title refers to the traditional days off for domestics, and it is significant because it shifts attention away from their working hours to their time off—to spaces of autonomy and independent lives. Thursdays and every other Sunday gave back to domestic workers a bit of their humanity. The book's articulation of the politics of dissent, resistance, and subversion dispels the myths and misconceptions that buttressed the exploitation of Black servants. The belief that African American women were content and loyal domestic workers was part of the racialized constructions of Black womanhood that justified their status as household workers.

Thursdays and Every Other Sunday Off, at the moment of its publication and today, is a departure from much of the literature that has portrayed domestic workers alternately as happy appendages to white families, as victimized objects of pity, or as evil incarnate. Smart-Grosvenor offers a vastly more nuanced and empowering view of domestic work. As she demonstrates, domestic workers were not voiceless. They may have been muted, but they were not voiceless. She simply unmuted them. Reviewing the history of domestic work will illuminate the power of her intervention.

A Brief History of Domestic Work

In the early twentieth century, domestic work was one of the few occupations open to African American women and was weighted with a long history of slavery, servitude, and racial oppression.[1] In 1900 Black women constituted 28 percent of domestic workers; by 1950 they were 60 percent.[2] Black women labored in the homes of

[1] See, for example, Bonnie Thornton Dill et al., "For the Good of Family and Race: Gender, Work, and Domestic Roles in the Black Community, 1880–1930," *Signs* 15, no. 2 (Winter 1990): 336–49.
[2] Susan B. Carter et al., *Historical Statistics of the United States: Earliest Times to the Present* (New York: Cambridge University Press, 2006), Table Ba1061–74, "Major Occupational Groups—Females: 1860–1990"; Table Ba1103–16, "Major Occupational Groups—White Females: 1860–1990"; and Table Ba1117–30, "Major Occupational Groups—Nonwhite Females: 1860–1990."

white southerners, serving a cultural as well as economic function. Their subordination was both a result of and reinforced by white racial power. Exploited economically and sexually, Black women's assertions of humanity and independent family life were circumscribed by predatory white male employers and white female employers who determined what they wore, what they ate, where they ate, which bathrooms they used, and the specific ways they carried out their responsibilities. The low pay, lack of benefits, long hours, and master–servant character of the relationship degraded the economic value of African American women's labor.

The period from the 1890s through the 1940s experienced a "Mammy craze," in the words of scholar Cheryl Thurber, in which the stereotype of a content and loyal African American servant who embodied a racial harmony was featured prominently in advertising, the arts, and literature.[3] White northerners and southerners attempted to put the divisiveness and resentment of the Civil War behind them and mask contemporary racial violence by romanticizing the "mammy" figure. For white Americans, the "mammy" became a source of comfort when racial strife was heightened and provided concrete evidence that the paternal southern order made African Americans happy.

Dominant white society used the stereotype of the "mammy" to justify African American women's status as household laborers and to reconstitute racial hierarchies. As historian Kimberly Wallace-Sanders puts it, "mammy" was "a code word for appropriately subordinate black behavior."[4] In 1936, Margaret Mitchell's novel *Gone with the Wind* generated a national commercial audience for the stereotyped figure; the character of Mammy is a caricatured, heavyset Black

[3] Cheryl Thurber, "The Development of the Mammy Image and Mythology," in *Southern Women: Histories and Identities*, ed. Virginia Bernard (Columbia: University of Missouri Press, 1992), 87–108; Grace Elizabeth Hale, *Making Whiteness: The Culture of Segregation in the South, 1890–1940* (New York: Vintage, 1999); Micki McElya, *Clinging to Mammy: The Faithful Slave in Twentieth-Century America* (Cambridge: Harvard University Press, 2007). See also Elizabeth Ross Haynes, "Negroes in Domestic Service in the United States: Introduction," *Journal of Negro History* 8, no. 4 (1923): 384–442 and K. Sue Jewell, *From Mammy to Miss America and Beyond: Cultural Images and the Shaping of U.S. Social Policy* (New York: Routledge, 1993).

[4] Kimberly Wallace-Sanders, *Mammy: A Century of Race, Gender, and Southern Memory* (Ann Arbor: University of Michigan Press, 2008), 106. Wallace-Sanders uses the phrase "mammy prism" to illustrate how the mammy figure reflected the broader politics of race.

servant who demonstrates unwavering loyalty to the O'Hara family over three generations. The astounding success of the book and film suggests how comfortable white Americans were with the idealized image of the Black maid.

In 1924, the United Daughters of the Confederacy, an organization of white southern women whose name implies a commitment to the vision of a slave South, launched a campaign to build a federally funded national "black mammy" monument in the nation's capital. African American activists, many of whom were involved in the New Negro cultural movement promoting racial pride, furiously opposed the congressional bill, claiming that the proposed monument glorified slavery and Black subservience.[5] For them the "mammy" figure was a distortion of the historical record, reflecting a paternalism that continued to shape domestic worker–employer relations into the twentieth century. African American activist Mary Church Terrell, one of the most outspoken opponents of the proposed monument, wrote that if it were built "there are thousands of colored men and women who will fervently pray that on some stormy night the lightning will strike it and the heavenly elements will send it crashing to the ground."[6] African American opposition to the legislation carried the day. The bill passed the Senate but died in the House, and the monument was never built. For the Black community, domestic service became a powerful symbol of racial exploitation and a platform for the assertion of Black women's rights. Middle- and working-class African Americans challenged both the constellation of ideas that associated African American women with household labor and the social and economic arrangements that confined African American women to this occupation.

ORGANIZING AND STORYTELLING AS RESISTANCE

Black domestic workers had a long history of organizing. They turned to both the legacy of slavery and the nature of their work to formu-

[5] Joan Marie Johnson, "'Ye Gave Them a Stone': African American Women's Clubs, Frederick Douglass, and the Black Mammy Monument," *Journal of Women's History* 17, no. 1 (2005): 62–86.
[6] Mary Church Terrell, *Washington (D.C.) Evening Star*, February 10, 1923. Quoted in Johnson, "'Ye Gave Them a Stone,'" 62.

late critiques of Black working-class life. They did not merely play a supportive role in the struggle for Black freedom but generated new tactics and nurtured new ideas of Black activism in resisting the fundamental arrangements of white supremacy.

In the 1930s, domestic workers such as Dora Jones in New York City confronted Depression-era conditions that relegated Black women domestics to informal day work, dubbed "slave markets" by Black journalists Ella Baker and Marvel Cooke. Jones established a hiring hall, fought for minimum wage protection, and pushed for higher standards. She was not alone. Domestic workers in Baltimore, Newark, and El Paso also mobilized.[7] In the 1960s and 1970s, in the context of civil rights and Black power, domestic workers established a nationwide movement. Geraldine Roberts in Cleveland formed the Domestic Workers of America in 1965. In Atlanta, Dorothy Bolden started the National Domestic Workers Union. Geraldine Miller and Carolyn Reed organized the Household Technicians in New York City, and Mary McClendon formed the Household Workers Organization in Detroit. With the help of an employer organization, the National Committee on Household Employment, these workers coalesced to form the first-ever national domestic workers' organization, the Household Technicians of America (HTA).

Storytelling, a hallmark feature of this book, was a key strategy used by domestic workers to build their movement. Domestic workers were not a natural political constituency, if there is any such thing. Storytelling became their way to connect with one another and to develop a base of solidarity. They shared stories about their mothers, aunts, grandmothers, and sisters. They shared their own stories of abuse and mistreatment, and they offered strategies for resistance and subversion. Geraldine Miller told stories she had heard about the Bronx Slave Market where employers drove by looking to hire for the day a woman with the most scarred knees because that was evidence

7 Esther Victoria Cooper, "The Negro Woman Domestic Worker in Relation to Trade Unionism" (MA thesis, Fisk University, 1940); Vanessa May, *Unprotected Labor: Household Workers, Politics, and Middle-Class Reform in New York, 1870–1940* (Chapel Hill: University of North Carolina Press, 2011); Tera W. Hunter, *To 'Joy My Freedom: Southern Black Women's Lives and Labors after the Civil War* (Cambridge: Harvard University Press, 1997).

that she scrubbed floors on her hands and knees. Miller told this story in disgust and anger to convey to other domestic workers that no one should ever have to scrub the floor down on all fours.[8]

Domestic workers were integral to the postwar struggle for Black freedom. It has almost become part of civil rights folklore to reference the aging domestic worker who chose to boycott buses in Montgomery and suffered from aching feet. They were the foot soldiers providing a necessary base for the burgeoning civil rights movement that propelled into leadership figures such as Martin Luther King Jr. Georgia Gilmore was one of those domestics. Living in Montgomery, Alabama, in the early 1950s, she initiated her own personal boycott of the buses because of ongoing harassment by bus drivers, well before Rosa Parks's celebrated moment. Once the boycott was in full swing, Gilmore dedicated herself to mobilizing the support of other domestic workers using her culinary skills. Gilmore recounted: "We collected $14 from amongst ourselves and bought some chickens, bread, and lettuce, started cooking and made up a bundle of sandwiches for the big rally. We had a lot of our club members who were hard-pressed and couldn't give more than a quarter or half-dollar, but all knew how to raise money. We started selling sandwiches and went from there to selling full dinners in our neighborhoods and we'd bake pies and cakes for people."[9]

Gilmore formed the Club from Nowhere, an organization of maids, service workers, and cooks. The veiled name was chosen to shield members from the consequences of supporting the boycott. The underground network of maids went door to door selling sandwiches, pies, and cakes and collecting donations; the proceeds were turned over to boycott leaders. The campaign spread, and soon Montgomery had several clubs across the city. They raised hundreds of dollars every week. Gilmore offered the money at the Monday-night mass meetings to wild cheers and thunderous applause. Georgia Gilmore, like so many other domestic workers of this period, evinced leadership and tangible strategic contributions to the struggle for Black freedom.

[8] Francis X. Clines, "About New York: Cleaning Women—Why Sit and Cry?" *New York Times*, June 22, 1978. Premilla Nadasen, *Household Workers Unite: The Untold Story of African American Women Who Built a Movement* (Boston: Beacon Press, 2015).
[9] Vernon Jarrett, "Raised Funds for Blacks: 'Club from Nowhere' Paid Way of Boycott," *Chicago Tribune*, December 4, 1975.

THURSDAYS AND EVERY OTHER SUNDAY OFF

In the midst of this movement, Smart-Grosvenor set out to write this book. First published in 1972, *Thursdays and Every Other Sunday Off* reflected a critical moment in the history of domestic worker organizing. Smart-Grosvenor conveyed the exploitation, betrayal, distrust, and abuse that permeated the occupation. She tackled the racialized images that underpinned domestic work, exploding the Mammy Myth and debasing such cherished American icons as Aunt Jemima and Uncle Ben. She recounted that celebrated Black figures such as Zora Neale Hurston and Madame C. J. Walker were once employed as domestics. The stories that Smart-Grosvenor included in this book resonate with the stories that were central to domestic worker organizing. She gave voice to the growing discontent among household workers. The book ends on a powerful note: it closes with a resignation letter from "Aisha (slave name, Beulah)" to "Ms. Anne" that chronicles years of mistreatment. Aisha informs her former employer that she has joined the United Maids Liberation Front and declares that she would be happy to return to work under certain conditions and with a written contract.

Smart-Grosvenor also spoke to the vast gulf between middle-class white employers seeking feminist liberation and Black domestic workers. The mainstream women's movement in the 1970s preached the virtues of liberating oneself from the daily grind of housework and finding employment outside the home. Most of these feminists resorted to hiring poorer women of color to carry out their household responsibilities, creating not just distance but a dependent relationship between middle-class women's liberation and poor women's exploitation.

Despite the rich history of domestic worker organizing, public consciousness is still not primed to acknowledge or embrace the outspoken, militant, or demanding household worker. Even when household workers' exploitation and victimization are fully exposed, they are rarely seen as agents of change. Kathryn Stockett's *The Help*, for example, brings to light the ways in which Black domestic service was embedded in racialized southern culture. She elevates the humanity of Black domestic workers and draws attention to racial mistreatment, but Stockett ultimately relies on a white protagonist—an employer, no less—who must step in and speak on behalf of the dis-enfranchised.[10] Although *The Help* is situated at a time when Black domestic workers were a national force, Stockett manages to erase this history and undercut the power and agency of workers.

This new edition of Smart-Grosvenor's book comes during a re-surgence of domestic worker organizing. *Thursdays and Every Other Sunday Off* contributes a critical analysis of the legacy of slavery and racism that permeates the occupation. Household service today is populated largely by immigrant women of color and is structured around the inequalities of language, immigration status, ethnicity, and race. The National Domestic Workers Alliance has launched the We Dream in Black project to highlight the plight of Black house-hold workers. Much like it was in the 1970s, the status of household labor is deeply intertwined with the larger conversation about racial and gender inequality.

Vertamae Smart-Grosvenor had a long and multifaceted career dedicated to empowering the marginalized. She called herself a "cu-linary griot" and was simultaneously a food critic, chef, journalist, actress, author, activist, anthropologist, and NPR commentator. A na-tive of South Carolina, her classic *Vibration Cooking: or, The Travel Notes of a Geechee Girl* (1970), part cultural history, part cookbook, celebrated the virtues of Gullah food, reclaiming what many felt was a maligned culture. If Smart-Grosvenor were to write a rap today, it would undoubtedly speak to the growing expansion of the service industry, the way race continues to determine one's status, and the notorious instances of violence and abuse. She would cogently distill the essence of racial and class inequality as it manifests in paid house-hold labor. But she would also give voice to the politics of resistance.

10 Kathryn Stockett, *The Help* (New York: Penguin Publishing Group, 2009).

I

"All in a day's work . . ."

Before you ask, I'll tell you why I chose the title *Thursdays and Every Other Sunday Off*. Cause that's what they used to give you.

"Thursdays and every other Sunday will be your days off": with these words for years many of our mothers, sisters, aunts, cousins and friends entered domestic life.

Either you did days work and got $5.00 and carfare, or you slept in and had Thursdays and every other Sunday off.

My mother did days work and, because of me, never took no sleep-in jobs, but other people in my family have. And it's not over yet. I got a cousin who is working on her Master's at the University of South Carolina, and she works every summer for a family in Connecticut. They don't even know that she's been to college. They love her because "she is so intelligent and takes all the phone messages properly." She says that she hopes this summer will be her last. "I hope to God I won't never have to lay eyes on them bukras again."

Ever notice a weird thing about days work? It's always the other side of town—suburbia or the hills. Don't nobody be working down the block. Cross the country there are bus stops and train routes that transport people going to servant. On the number 44 bus in Philadelphia or the Shaker Rapid in Cleveland, the Bexley or Upper Arlington bus in Columbus or the Penn Central in New York. It's the domestic line.

I rode the Penn Central into Westchester and I was moved and mad. At 125th Street nothing but sisters get on. Going to work for

Miss Anne. Riding the domestic train. I sometimes wonder if that 125th Street was put on just to "accommodate" Miss Anne.

I heard the sisters talking on the train:

"That hussy want me to work late today. She meeting a friend for a late lunch. She meeting some man in a motel, cause I heard her making the rangements."

"When I was in the den, he come in and put his hand on my behind, telling me, you gaining weight."

"That brat of hers is the one on that _____ commercial. They making plenty money off that stupid kid."

"No, he don't know she drink. She hide the bottles in a empty Kotex box and he too shy to look in there. White women is tricky."

"Mine don't know she drink either. She start drinking soon as he leave. By lunch she is drunk as a sailor in port after three months on sea."

"That new baby don't look nothing like him."

"Asked me could I work next week when that Blumstein kid gets Bar Mitzvah'd. I told her no, ask Pearl Sanders. *Shoot*, I can't stand working them parties. A room full of whitefolks makes me nervous."

"She used to give beautiful clothes. Now she got so she wanna sell them to me. I told her there was plenty thrift stores in my neighborhood, if and when I get ready to buy second-hand clothes. It just didn't seem right, a blouse that I have been washing and ironing for years, I got to wind up paying for. White people must think we aint got no sense."

"I keep telling her I gonna leave cause my son need me to take care of his children, and she keep saying, oh, please wait until I find someone to replace you. I can't manage with no help.

Shit, this week's my last. She will manage the way she managed before I got there."

The cities change. The bus line is different. The train runs on another track, but the scene is the same. Everyday in America, South Africa and other places in the world like them. Black People. My people. Travelin. To be cooks, janitors, housekeepers, porters, days workers, servants, Black boys, Beige girls, Brown daddies, Ebony mothers.

*EbonyMothers**

I

The mighty hawk whipped their long dark coats
into a regal cloud about them
high above the hotjunkies and nodding
tricksisters
searching for some hollow frozen revenge

The sun sparkled from their shining ebonyfaces
reflecting a more glorious future
as the penncentral squeezed into one two five
sucking them up to
plain whiteplains
where funny little snowgirls
dream of suntans and mantans

the whiterythym of the train forced
ebonymothers to talk of Miss Ann's
latest stupidities
but for all the sisters this day
was their last—as all the other days

the ajax and joy tried for the millionth time
to bleach their ebonyhands
as the missus house burst
blackclean

* *EbonyMothers* copyright © 1972 by S. E. Anderson. Printed by permission of the author.

like the syncopated moves of tina turner
they all struck a match at noon
like a chorus of 1000 nina's
they all moaned into the phone:
fire, fire everywhere, the house is burnin down!

Like 1000 aunt jemimas they all ran close
to hug miss ann
holdin her tight cryin watchin the burnin house

like 1000 beulahs they drew close
                    they drew their hatpins
                    they drew deathblood
from the screamin miss anns
all over plain white plains

with shoppinbags packed with more than
the usual goodies
our ebonymothers boarded ol' penncentral
with smiles dyin to tell of the fires
in their hearts
of the fires in their miss ann's home

II

Their children waited for a tired bent mother to return
What will they say when Moms comes home more relaxed
than ever?
what will park ave & one two five
do in the morning sunrise
when there are no ebonymothers goin north?

What will mr. ann do when he returns home
to ashes blood and a silent screaminface
of miss ann?
what will the snowbrats do with no TV?

What will *you* do to make the revolution come?

Ebonymothers' eyes are upon you

S. E. Anderson, 8/71

What's a domestic? The dictionary says "a hired household servant." A servant is defined as being a person employed in domestic duties.

New York *Times*, October 15, 1970:

The domestic household worker was described yesterday as "the most exploited woman in America" because she is ineligible for protection of the minimum-wage laws, has no health insurance or job security and often receives less than $60 for a 60-hour week. . . .

. . . Of the one and a half million domestics, 82 per cent had cash incomes of less than $2,000 a year, and 57 per cent less than $1,000, according to a United States Labor Department study.

Hundreds of thousands of them are heads of households with families who rely on them. Housework will never be lucrative, but it should be decently paid and secure.

. . . a woman who said she had been "lured" to New York from her family's farm in North Carolina by an advertisement that promised "$50 a week with your own room and TV."

The woman, Mrs. Patricia Jones, a 30-year-old teachers' aide at Public School 225 in Brooklyn, said: "I was making only $20 a week at the time, so of course I jumped at the opportunity."

Although Mrs. Jones's experience occurred in 1958, she returned to the same agency this summer [Summer '70] looking for work, she said, and encountered "the same situation—nothing had changed."

The employment agency sent her a bus ticket, she said, and within two weeks she was sitting in the New York office where "well-married white women were walking up and down looking at all of us trying to choose."

"It was like a slave market and they said things like, 'She can't speak proper English. I don't want her around my children,' and 'She's too dirty, I don't want her in my home.'"

She said she got a live-in job for $30 a week, six days a week, 7 A.M. to 11 P.M. caring for a 14-room house and two children.

"Not knowing any better," Mrs. Jones said, "and being used to the slave-labor practices of the South, I assumed that the way the domestics were being traded and abused was a normal part of getting a job."

The same day I saw that piece in the paper I was walking on Fifth Avenue. I saw a white man cleaning a building. The dude was wiping doorknobs, cleaning windows, sweeping etc. The friend I was walking with said "see that white man doing 'menial' work." Well 10 times out of 12 it's not considered menial. Don't nobody call him the janitor and I bet you he makes some good bucks, liability plus seniority, social security insurance and all the other benefits. Plus he's got a title. He's called "Director of Property Maintenance." Maintenance, housekeeping department, home technicians usually mean white—benefits and good pay. Domestic usually means colored—low and no benefits. It's all in the name?

Who wants to sleep in your house and be called on 24 hours a day? Cause that's what sleeping in is all about.

When the W.F.'s[1] hire you, sure you have your own room, T.V. and your Thursdays and every other Sunday off, but after you finish cooking and serving the dinner, washing the dinner dishes, and putting the kids to bed, you're too tired to hardly think about getting the train or bus into town. You can't go out to the cocktail lounge for a drink. Did you ever see a domestic hanging out in the evening in your local cocktail lounge?

A friend of mine who has a one-woman show of poetry readings, told me that she once did a show in Great Neck, N.Y., for domestics who worked out there. It was sponsored by a group of Great Neck employers who wanted to bring cullud culture to their girls rather than have the girls go into "wicked Harlem" and look for it.

Serving and slaving is pretty much the same cross country. Give a bit more here and take a lot more there. East, West, Midwest, it really is not about locale it's about how you're treated. Always waiting on other people and taking care of their babies for a little money and no respect aint no play pretty.

I don't wanna hear about how much money they make. They don't make enough—to stay home and wipe the snot from their own children's nose. They don't make enough to have a woman come in while they go to work. I wanna ask this question—whether you sleep in, do days work, or semi-weekly domestic work—Is there enough money to rent a slave? Cause that's what it is. How much do it cost to

[1] W.F.'s stands for whitefolks.

get someone in to wash your stinking drawers, rock your crying baby, and take your orders? Is there enough money to send for a girl from the South or the Islands, or, as of late, South America, to keep house for you, mind your overindulged brat, while you go to Women's Lib meetings? Tell me. Take a girl out of her culture, have her work for you with no way out, no future except to be one of your family—by feeling, not marriage, and if she goes, get another "darkie" to replace her?

Is there enough money for that?

How much do that cost? $30.00 a week? $10.00 a day? $1.50 an hour? $0.75 an hour?

They rung my bell to ask me could I recommend a maid. I said, yes, your mama.[2]

Langston Hughes

Housework has always been the thing. When I was a little girl, I never knew that Black women could have any other job (cepting show biz).

One day in grammar school we had a Black substitute teacher and the class was disrupted. I went to school in Philadelphia, Francisville section, the Lydia Darrah Elementary School. At that time, the principal, the nurse, the teachers, were All White. The school student body was "integrated," about 60% white and 40% Black.

Oddly enough, we used to sing the Negro National Anthem, "Lift Every Voice and Sing," by James Weldon Johnson, every morning—after The Lord's Prayer and "Oh, Say Can You See."

Anyhow, most of us were the sons and daughters of women in "service," doing days work or whatever name you wanna call it, but most of our mothers were working in W.F.'s homes.

Some of the younger teachers in the school were newly married, and their husbands were doing graduate work and they were living off their teacher's salary, couldn't afford a "regular" woman to clean so they used the older girls in the school on Saturday.

I worked for a teacher, regularly on Saturdays for a few months (until my father found out). I was in the fifth grade. She lived in West Philadelphia in a three-room apartment. I thought it was a

[2] Langston Hughes, *Ask Your Mama*. New York: Knopf, 1961, p. 47. Copyright © 1959, 1961 by Langston Hughes. Reprinted by permission of Alfred A. Knopf, Inc.

high-class apartment building and a fabulous apartment. Looking back, it was a lower middle class building in the University of Pennsylvania area. The apartment itself was quite ordinary. But at the time, to me it was great to be able to turn on hot and cold running water, clean the pretty bathroom, vacuum the carpet (cheap), and eat anything in the refrigerator. We had an icebox.

I had to take a trolley car and bus to get to her house and she would usually drive me home. I worked from 9 to about 1 P.M. for 50¢ an hour. If she went out shopping, I'd read the magazines and look at the books.

My mother made me take a bath, put on clean underwear (in case something happened on the way and I had to go to the hospital), and she would plait my hair on Friday nights and I'd sleep with a stocking cap so it would be nice cause I was working for a teacher.

Some of the other girls in the school worked too. We would compare notes and talk about how whose house was and what they ate and how much we were getting. We all lied about the money part. I said I was getting 75¢ an hour and didn't have to do nothing but vacuum the floor, wax the kitchen and dust the furniture with a feather duster and eat anything I wanted. We told lies about whose "employer" had the most and prettiest clothes. I guess we felt that the "higher class" the employer, the better we were. "Employees" always do that. Have you noticed that sales people in "high class" department stores are snobs? I felt bad one time I went to Bendel's to buy some shoes and the woman looked at my feet (checking out the shoes I was wearing), asked my size (10), took ⅓ of a minute to tell me that she didn't have any style of any shoe in Shoe Biz my size. I felt awful. It had taken me all morning to dress "right" and a great deal of courage to even venture inside Bendel's. So, I said fuck it to myself—and went to Klein's, found some leather-bottoms-and-man-made-upper shoes for $6.99.

When I get rich and famous I think I'm gonna get me a maid just to wash dishes and the bathtub.

I love cooking, but I don't like washing the dishes, and as far as the bathtub is concerned, it is a drag to bend down and try to get it clean.

I've never lived anywhere with a sho nuff *Clean A-1 bathroom*. The tubs have always had permanent rings. Ajax, Bon Ami, Clorox, Mex could not wash them away.

In one place the tub was so dingy I felt dirty when I got out of the tub. It was very depressing. I got some epoxy paint and painted it a bright sun yellow. It was beautiful while it lasted, but the sun set and it was as ugly as ever. For once I want to live in a place with a bathroom that is *first class*. As a matter of fact, I aint never lived in a house that wasn't halfway deteriorated. I am tired of moving in, painting, scraping paint off the floors and walls, building book shelves on the walls that were warped, hanging pictures and paintings[3] over cracks.

One morning my daughter Kali stepped out of the bathroom and the ceiling fell. I called the landlord (after I hugged my child) and said, "Listen, I told you that the bathroom ceiling was leaking. The people on the 2nd and 3rd floor told you. For the past eighteen months all that water has been settling, and this morning at 7:10 the mutha fucker fell and cracked the toilet, knocked the sink down, put a hole in the floor. Do you know what it would have done to my child?" He said, "Hold on, don't get upset. I'll send the boy[4] over this afternoon.

I've paid the dues required to "rough it." I've seen that I can move into a dump and creatively make it a livable place. Now let's see how I would do if I could *start* with straight, clean walls. Would all my soul go down the gutter if I had a decent bathroom?

I wanna find out, cause I am fed up with all this.

When I move this time, I am changing up. Nevermore will I go to the liquor store to get boxes to move. I'm gonna get the Acme Moving Company to pack my books, pictures, and paintings. I want the Acme Moving Company cause in all the movies, books, etc., Acme is always the company. I'll pack my own clothes—aint too many of them going, either. And I'm walking out.

I'm walking out "in the sunshine." And when I move in my new apartment, I'm gonna get me a white cleaning lady. That may seem strange to some of yall, but after all the years my mama spent on her knees, it would make me sick to have anyone in her image cleaning my house.

[3] I may be poor but I aint culturally deprived.
[4] a Black man about 30.

It's bad enough that the "are you the maid?" syndrome is still around.

One fall day in '65 I was walking down First Ave., feeling good. I had just made my first Vogue Couturier pattern, and found a shoe store that didn't blink me out cause I wore size 10 shoe. I was wearing the suit and the shoes. I knew that I was fly. I was on my way to Stuyvesant Town to pick up my daughter, who was visiting a little girl in her class. I was thinking, "I swanee. I done grew up." Cause I could remember when I was in kindergarten and my mama picked me up. It was the first time I started to think of me as somebody's mama and not just somebody's child.

First Ave. was pleasant. It was when I turned into Stuyvesant Town that the bad vibrations hit me. To start with, Stuyvesant Town is a citadel of white supremacy. It weren't built for no Black folks from the git. The few that got in is overcolored. Anyhow, I had the address and since all the buildings looked alike, I was confused. I asked a Black woman where Number 520 was, and she said you go in over there. I dug that she meant the service entrance, so I said no, the front. She said, "Oh, you going in for your first interview, huh?"

I decided not to deal with that and found the front entrance. As I was waiting for the elevator, a middle-aged white woman smiled at me and said, "Going in late today, aren't you?" "Huh," I said. "You are going in late today, aren't you?" "Miss," I said, "I am not a maid. I am going to pick up my daughter who is visiting a classmate. All of us aren't maids, you know." "Oh, well, we do get a lot of good ones down here."

The elevator came and we got in. Thinking that it was better not to say anything to the woman, and that my ice would get her, I settled in a corner of the elevator and decided to find out what apartment I wanted when I got to my floor. I rolled my eyes at her and reached into my huge purse to find the slip of paper and happened to look up, and what to my wondering eyes did I see—the old lady in the corner of the elevator, crying! She thought that when I reached into my purse and rolled my eyes at her I was going to get my knife, and if you doubt my analysis of the situation, dig what she said to me: "Take everything, but please don't hurt me." I shook my head this time and got off at 11—went to find D or C, I can't remember which, and rang the bell. Mrs. All-American, with whom I had let my child spend the afternoon, said, "Did you have any trouble finding us?" I smiled and said, "A few traumas, but no trouble."

"Huh?"

It's a common thing for colored folks to be told by a doorman to go to the service entrance. What is a service entrance? How come the people who wash your clothes, cook your food, care for your child got to enter a separate door? Does the doormat man use the service entrance? Last time a doorman told me to use the service entrance I told him to tell it to his mama.

Guards—Doormen—House Dicks of all kinds are always stopping colored people. A friend of mine who is looking for a job told me the other day that he wanted to put in an application at CBS but couldn't get by the guard. It even happened to me. One time I went to Doubleday to pick up something, and I'd left home in a hurry. I wasn't fly (but I wasn't looking scroungy). My head was tied up with a head rag—not a gele. I had on a dress that wasn't too fashionable—on the other hand it wasn't that bad. I asked the receptionist if there was a package, and she say, "No." I said, "Are you sure?" "Yeah," she says. I told her that less than forty-five minutes ago I'd been told that the package was left and would be at her desk in a manila envelope. Just then I spotted it, and at the same time I dug that she hadn't even asked me my name! What was happening was just cause I was a non-fashionable looking Black, she didn't feel she had to deal with me. I asked her again and she looked up from her book in annoyance as if to say, "Are you still here?" and said, "I told you it is not here." Just then Carol Parks, an assistant editor, came along and I said, "How come yall make me come all the way up here and aint no package?" Carol said, "I left it right here with the receptionist. There it is."

The receptionist looked fit to be tied, but I wouldn't have tied her. That wasn't no victory for me. She just took all my energy.

Happens all the time. I went to the store to buy typing paper to finish this book and the woman assumed I was a maid buying paper for my madam and insisted that I get a receipt so the madam would have proof of the cost. Black people—obviously to that woman, don't need white typing paper.

They do housework and run errands for W.F.'s. Watch some nigger-studier come along and tell me I've got the situation all wrong. It had nothing to do with me being Black. "That lady was an exception, just one incident but not typical of W.F.'s feelings towards Blacks." How come I got to keep on understanding and believing that every time I am in a situation that puts me through changes, it's not real or typical, it's just that I have run into exceptional whites.

Will the real whites stand up, please!! Stand! I wanna see you so I know you when I meet you.

Hey you look familiar. You look like the teacher in the movie *Imitation of Life*, who said that there was no colored in the school, when Peola's momma came with her galoshes, and you resemble that lady at the Thrift Store who told me to "bring the carriage in the store 'in case the owner passes by and thinks you are goofing off'" when I was out shopping with my daughter. And you must be kin to that dude who had the nerve to tell me on the day that my phone was cut off, my purse was snatched, Angela Davis celebrated her 27th birthday in jail, the hospital informed me that Kali's broken arm was set wrong but could be corrected with rehabilitation, a junkie next door O.D.'d and was tossed off the roof right in our backyard, "The trouble is that you are hypersensitive, nervous and uptight."

I remember when the Lion of Judah, Haile Selassie, gave Jackie Kennedy a leopard coat. Well, seems like the day she wore it on the front page of the *Daily News*, was the same day I was wearing my fake leopard. So there I am styling on Orchard Street, wearing my fake leopard, big bell bottom pants (in those days wasn't nobody wearing big bell bottom pants cepting me and Kadjeha), a purple velour sweater with a hat to match that I'd made. I know I was fly (W.F.'s say chic). Anyhow, there I was, shopping for fabric so I could make more fly outfits. I was doing my thing. The man in the store commented on how I looked and likened my coat to Jackie's. "No," said I, "hers was a gift and it is the real McCoy. I bought mine and it's a fake." O.K., so I buy my fabric and am ready to leave the store, and the man says, "You look very much like Jackie Kennedy. You look beautiful. Please, take my card." I looked at him. I don't hardly look like Jackie. My hair aint never near that long. I take the card, turn to go out the door, and notice the dude has got his hand in his fly and is foaming at the mouth and says in a husky voice, "Please call me soon, maybe you do a little housework for me."

Then there was the time I was in Copenhagen in a shop, buying sweaters for the girls, and a white couple from the Bronx went into their act. The girls and I are doing our thing—not too much—just doing it easy like, and Mr. & Mrs. Spencer llowed, "That sweater is adorable, really stunning. It's good looking, a smart number." I didn't ask her, right? She goes on and on. "I'm Mrs. Spencer from the Bronx and this is my husband, Mr. Spencer, and we were just commenting on how much you look like Gladys, the girl who works for us." I didn't buy the sweaters. I grabbed the girls and left.

W.F.'s got a bad habit of making free like that. Just come up and start talking to you bout all kind foolish things. What annoys me is that they think that if they feel like talking to you, you feel like it.

Lessen you think it's just me taking these trips, let me tell you about my friend who

> look like a queen
> walk like a queen
> talk like a queen

and is a sho nuff queen of the universe, says that she was in the make-up room of a major network show and a bookwriter came in and started talking.

Says he: I don't use much make-up.
Says she: Pity.
He: Just a little blush.
She: I can dig where you coming from.
He: Try the #76 that worked good last time.
She: Try what and when?
He: Are you Pauline, the make-up girl?
She: 9 ★ * # * # *

While working on this project all I could think of was maids. Maids was on my mind. I asked friends to send me notes, letters, clippings—anything on the subject. A friend in Atlanta sent me a clipping from the Baltimore *Afro-American* about a maid in Philadelphia who chopped off her employer's head and was found cleaning the ax off in the sink. She was bloody well arrested.

Another friend sent me a clipping from *Jet* magazine with a note that said, "Miss Mae, here's something for you on Space Maids."

BLACK MAIDS PROTEST SPACE RACE SPENDING

Unable to understand why the U.S. squanders billions in the space race, when millions of people in this country go hungry daily, a group of black maids who earn about $35 a week cleaning hotel rooms marched 75 miles from Daytona Beach, Fla. to Cape Kennedy on the eve of the Apollo 14 Moon Launch.[5]

Chuck and Barbara Hayes are friends of mine who served in the Peace Corps in India. Here's a letter from Barbara . . .

> Petliputra Colony
> Patna, Bihar
> India
> April, 1968

Dear Verta,

What's happening, girl? Lord, do we miss Manhattan. Being here reminds me of that old rhyme: New York, New York; it's so nice they named it twice.

One thing I've learned for life—I sure ain't no country girl, and India is pure country—that is, where we live.

Yesterday it was 123.3 degrees in the shade, but we intend to keep on keepin' on. 'Course we ain't hangin' in here by ourselves; we got 7 servants helpin' us to get over.

We didn't start off wanting that many, but after we hired the cook, we found out that he wouldn't wash the pots and pans— he'd just cook. So we hired a boy to wash the pots and pans. Then the boy hipped us that he wouldn't sweep the kitchen floor; so we hired a sweeper to sweep all the floors, including the kitchen. Actually, we had a series of sweepers until we finally found one that would also clean bathrooms.

Later on we figured if we were going to keep our clothes clean we would have to hire a laundryman or Dhobi to wash and iron for us.

[5] *Jet* Magazine, February 17, 1971.

After some careful scrutinizing of the situation we concluded that the concept of the babysitter is in full swing in India, but only on a full-time basis. So we hired an Aya to look after Regan during my exits from the house.

Since we grow our own vegetables, we needed a Molle (gardener) to nurture the vegetables in the 120 degree sun—I tried this action once for ten minutes and just knew I was getting ready to say bye to this world; that's how sick I was behind it.

And last but not least, we hired a Chokidar or nightwatchman to guard the compound from 6 P.M. until 6 A.M. The robbers here are mean and they ain't lookin' for no fix—just aimin' to put you in one. Half the night the Chokidar marches around the house coughing and clearing his throat to let us know he is still "on duty."

Hey Verta, I'm on my 5th cook and my latest project is teaching him how to make potatoe salad.

I'll have to tell you about the dismissal of our 4th cook in my next go-round, 'cause ain't no way I could be objective if I told you now. However, I will venture to say that I was finally able to document my suspicions that the dude had T.B. so Chuck agreed to let him go. But I must admit that Mohammed did his thing for 3 weeks before he said his final "Namaste, Meme Sahib."

And I guess that's what I've been trying to say all through this letter—the Indians are masters at "doing your own thing."

Actually our housework is such that I could have organized it in such a way as to distribute it equally among 2 or 3 full-time servants at the most. But the Indians said no good and no thanks to your equal distribution of labor. We don't play that equality thing over here. So instead of supporting 2 or 3 Indian families indirectly, we were helping to feed and care for 7 families.

After analyzing the situation for a few months, I realized the Indians had a point. In doing their own thing and nothing but their own thing, they gave other Indians a chance to do their own thing and thus build up each other and their country.

I thought to myself, could this perhaps be the key to nation building; to do your own thing in such a way as to embrace and include your brother and not isolate and separate him? If it is a key, we better get some copies made and start opening our own doors.

I started to say see you later, but over here it's,

Namaste,

Barbara
or
(as my servants call me behind my back),

Barbara Meme Sahib

P.S. A respectful reference is just Meme Sahib.

I got a good friend in Sister Kay Lindsay. We've had good times and deep talks. Kay's a rapper and writer. Last year, she left New York. She traveled from Fun City to D.C. to Atlanta to New Orleans to Chicago back to D.C. trying to make it real.

In Chicago, Kay stayed at her Aunt Berlena's house and had a ball. Aunt Berlena is a poet in her eighties. When I told Kay about the domestic book I was doing she told me Aunt Berlena had a poem that was on that case.

Here's Kay's letter and the poem. . . .

Washington, D.C.
3 November 1970

As-Salaam-Alaikum:
Dear Sister,
I may yet be on Tee Vee. The story you told me about the guy who expected you to sing and had a small band, well its really funny. I expected to do a demo tape for radio and it was Tee Vee. If it comes through, well you will have to come down for an interview. Here is Aunt Berlena's poem:

EXHUR'S CHAT—A True Story
(Exhur's white folks)

Let me tell you bout my white folks
I worked fur twelve years or more
And you might as well believe it
Kase all of hit am so.

Mis Clarky and Capun Davis
Wus dem good folkses name
And de way I loved dem white folks
Hit railly wus a shame.

Da wus de besses christuns
Dat jined de baptis church
And rich as any cow cream
Da wus so very much.

Da had de finest chilluns
Dat ever walked de earth
Da wus so rich and up to date
Know dat wus in da birth.

Dare wus Mis Nora Cambel
Mis Stella and Mis Gert
Masse John T. Davis Jr., Masse Charley
And Mis Bert.

And when da come to see da parents
Let me tell you my chile
De vittes I'd put befo dem
Would make dem chilluns smile.

Dat good ole greasy turkey
Dat good ole cream and cake
And specially dem transparent custards
Mis Clarky lunt me to make.

Mis Clarky and Captun Davis
Wus blessed frum head to toe
Wif de sweetest little gran chilluns
Bout twenty-five or mo.

Mis Clarky and dem wus good to me
Da allus had a smile
Aldo I wus de servant
l felt lak Ise de chile.

De Lord blessed dem wif ole age too
Da wus so good and kind
Da tried so hard to do good deeds
And leave none undone behind.

When da wus married fifty years
All er dem chilluns wus dare
Da had de golden wedden
Twus so fine I declare.

Da got de finest presents
All all er dem wus gold
I saw dat wif my own eyes
And not dat I wus told.

I don't git tired ob talking
Ob dat good ole sumtin' t'et (to eat)
I cooked hit wif dese here ole hands
And hit wus fit to eat.

But bye and bye sad times come
I hated hit so bad
I hate to talk about hit now
Hit make me feel so sad.

Mis Clarky died and lef us
God tuck yer home to dwell
All do we grieved behine her
But God does all things well.

She went way up in heaven
And stud dare bye de gate
Waiting for Captun Davis
She knowed he wouldn't be late.

And atter while Capun Davis died
Becase his time had come
Mis Clarky met him at de gate
And led him to de throne.

I knows hit wus a jolly time
When dem two angels met
I gwine up dare to wait on dem
But I ain't ready yet.

But dar's one consolation
Way in de bye and bye
Dar'll be a great reunion
Ob dat family in de sky.

                              Berlena White Mooney

Like I told you, she wrote this in sarcastic response to her sister
Exhur who was constantly talking about the people she worked
for. Now it so happened that this particular family had a little
money, maybe a lot, but you will have to get the details from
Aunt Ber. Anyway, when the old man died, he failed to remember
Exhur in his will. But she kept talking about them just the same.
When Aunt Ber wrote the poem and showed it to Aunt Exhur,
she took it to the surviving children, who wept copiously and
gave her some land and a house as recompense. This was in
Alabama I believe. Aunt Exhur eventually left the South for
Philly and asked the family to sell the property which they did

and then they sent her the sale money. Aunt Berlena tells it better though. When I told her that you were interested in her poems, she got them all out and we went over them (She's a Leo). When I typed them (they were all handwritten) she dug seeing them in "print". She is really beautiful, not pious, self-righteous, just beautifully real and funny and she knows she's got a crazy sense of humor.

                    Love,

                       Kay

P.S. Send her the proofs as soon as you can. She would really enjoy that—(Can you dig where I'm comin' from?)

I have a cousin named Madafwa, who is a Yamasee. Madafwa does not like people to call him a Yamasee Indian. Yamasees is. Indians aint. Madafwa also says Black instead of Negro. National Liberation Front instead of Viet Cong. Creek instead of Seminole. He has traveled all over the U.S.A. and I asked him to comment on "The Indian servant problem" if there was one.

Here's his letter. . . . .

My dearest cousin and most admired sister,

You asked me to comment on "Indian Servants." Firstly, I ain't never been one. I try to avoid working anyhow and I sure ain't gonna work for no Americans in their home. But my friend, Suelana, will be writing you. She is on that case in New Mexico and Arizona. My comments may not be too up-to-date but from what I've observed, a lot of Americans seem afraid to have an "Indian" that close to them. Plus they would rather work yall, makes them feel bigger and better. You think they got a guilt complex when it comes to yall? How you think they feel when they look at us. I imagine they must not feel too bad cause they ain't giving it back.

I was on Alcatraz, but I had to cut to the mainland and get a J.O.B. I worked in San Francisco as a combination bus/waiter and all around boy.

Before I got the job the bitch in Personnel went through a lot of changes trying to figure out my ethnic code. You know they don't just come right out now and write race any more. Its about codes. Don't you think America has entered the Code Age? (Zip, area, etc.)? Back to the bitch, she says to me, "Are you of Puerto Rican descent?" "Nope," I said. Smiling and frowning at the same time, she said, "You do resemble one you know." I said, "Yeah, a lot peoples say that." As I was talking, I could tell that my southern accent took her on a trip, concerning my geographical background.

"Are you a creole?" said the lady. "Nope—Yamasee."

"What's your race, you're hard to identify. I don't know what you are. Black, white or other" she shouted.

So I shouted, "Yamasee, like Navaho, Apache, like Geronimo, Yamasee."

"Oh, I see" she said, "You're an Indian."

Give everybody my love.

Write on,

Madafwa

P.S. ain't you glad Bobby's free

My friend Sharon sent me the following letter:
Dear Verta:

Hope the book is coming along. I've told you all I know, except the story my mother tells me about umbrellas. A friend of my mother's showed her an advertisement from a Baltimore newspaper (late 1920's or early 1930's) which had a cartoon of a mammy exclaiming "Lawd, de rain, de rain!" The advertisement urged people to get umbrellas for their mammys so they wouldn't be late for work because of rain. It mentioned that the umbrella came in "Cook's own colors, Black, Brown and Purple."

I met a brother from South Africa, and asked him about the domestic situation there. Some of the things he said reminded me of your rap. You know what you are always saying about how W.F.'s (see, you got me doing that) love to call you out your name. He was saying how the thing about names is the same the world over. I had mentioned that if a Black man has a Biblical name like Ezekiel, his white employer might not want to deal with that and will call him Mike or Shorty, or whatever. And the brother from South Africa said it's the same there, except that the South African brothers are all given the same name: Jack. The white people like to use it especially if they have company to the house. It will be "Jack, do this," "Jack, do that." And Emanuel, or Barney, or Ezekiel will have to answer to the name of Jack. The South African brother was saying that it's the same for Black women there. They're all Marie.

The brother told me that the maids there are virtually slaves. The cops come to the girls rooms at any time. The rooms are usually on the top floor and the "family" never goes up there. The cops go looking for the husband or boy friend. They figure you are not supposed to have a man anyway. If you want a husband, you can't work. The cops have master keys to the maid's rooms. They don't even knock—just kick the door open with their boots. A large percentage of the coloreds are children of the maids.

The brother told me a funny story . . . "One always does what Baas (Master or Boss) tells him to do. One kitchen boy was told by his master to go get AMAGANDA (eggs), but the master couldn't pronounce the click and said AMAKANDA (head). The boy did as he told, but said to himself 'Baas is crazy.' When master returned home, he found well cooked chicken heads."

Love,

Sharon

P.S. Enclosed is a clipping from the New York *Times*. Maybe it will be helpful to you.

New York *Times*, October 20, 1970:

It is black women who suffer most under the mass of legislation and regulations that underlie the Government's policy of apartheid or separate racial development. . . .

. . . Since black labor is necessary to white industry, African men are allowed to remain in white areas conditionally, preferably as contract labor without family or as "bachelors" in hostels.

Black women and children are officially considered "superfluous appendages," and more and more are being forced to go to the black "homelands"—poor, undeveloped areas set aside by the Government.

Here in western Cape Province the restrictions on women are the most severe because the authorities have declared that they do not want a permanent black population. Job priorities have been given to the Cape coloreds, or mulattoes, and businesses have been ordered to reduce black employment by 5 per cent yearly.

Labor shortages are such that industry and farmers are being forced to seek African laborers to replace coloreds, who are being admitted to semiskilled jobs usually held by whites. But there is greater official pressure to get black women and children out.

There are two black townships in the Capetown municipality with a total population of 81,000 in 1968, of whom 25,000 were women. The trend toward a population of men has been accentuated in the last two years.

The Athlone Advice Office reported hearing 1,800 cases last

year, concerning family groups and individuals seeking a way
to resist official pressure for resettlement. . . .

"Great wrongs are being perpetrated upon African women,"
it [Black Sash, a white women's volunteer group] declared in a
recent appeal. . . . The main abuses listed are:

Women are prevented from living with their husbands who
work in white urban areas.

Wives of contract laborers can see their husbands only once
a year for a couple of weeks at the end of a contract. They live
in unnatural communities, where there are only other women,
children and old people.

Working women in urban areas must send their children to
rural relatives; the children then lose all right to reside in urban
areas.

Under the widely criticized Urban Areas Act, no black woman
may remain in an urban area for more than 72 hours unless she
can prove that she has lived there continuously since birth, or
for a continuous period of 15 years, or for 10 years working for
one employer. . . .

The main job of the Athlone Advice Office, which is largely
manned by volunteers, is to explain the complicated rulings
that regulate the black South African's life and to try to help
him cope as well as possible. Black Sash also runs Advice Offices
in Durban and Johannesburg. . . .

Most of the cases concern couples that cannot reside together.
There was the young, happily married couple with one child
that had been ordered to separate. The only solution to the
problem is divorce, according to the Advice Office. Once di-
vorced, the woman can remain with an aunt as the unmarried
daughter of a Capetown resident and can see her "bachelor"
husband from time to time.

While the tragic parade of broken families passes through
the Advice Offices, separate development has not achieved its
aims.

The 1970 census recently made public, demonstrates the Government's failure to establish racially separate societies. Of a
black population of about 15 million, there are some eight million registered in white areas, or twice as many as the white
population. When the Government began separate development in 1951, there were five million blacks in white areas.

II

The
Domestics
Rap*

* NOTE: These are true stories. Only the names have been changed, to keep the faith and avoid embarrassment.

Lots of W.F.'s have asked their "help" to sign contracts not to write books on what they saw and heard while they were working in service. Since I got a penchant for being different, I decided to sign a contract to tell what we have seen working in service for some 300 odd years. I decided to do that after I realized that it was not Beulah, Hattie Mae or Aunty Mamie who wrote about their experiences . . . but white women who described them. Like *Soul Sister*, the female version of *Black Like Me*, by Grace Halsell.

Soul Sister is "the story of a white woman who turned herself black and went to live and work in Harlem and Mississippi." Grace blackens up in Puerto Rico, suffers through Harlem, rests in the Virgin Islands, and crusades through Mississippi to find out, write, and legitimatize what we Black women have been saying all along.

Grace Halsell writes about it, and she will probably go cross-country lecturing on "the Role of the Black women in Contemporary Society."

What I mean is, would you take as truth an elephant's account of what it's like to be a gazelle?

The most outrageous rip off is Beatrice Sandler's *African Cookbook*. After being brought here from Africa to cook, 300-odd years later a white woman is sent back to Africa to find out what we were cooking before we came.

Mrs. Sandler took a standard set of luggage, a satchel full of swivel-bladed paring knives, a tape recorder, her niece, and her ego, and went to Ethiopia, Ghana, Liberia, Kenya, and Tanzania, and came back with a "satchel full of recipes."

In a New York *Times* interview, September 17, 1970, Mrs. Sandler says:

"The idea for the African cookbook came about during the New York World's Fair when I was engaged for menu-planning for the African Pavilion. I worked on the menus for three months with people from all over Africa." . . .

"A somewhat limited cookbook came out of those discussions, and then World Publishing decided that what the world needed was a more extensive volume" Mrs. Sandler was furnished with an advance and an itinerary planned.

"The best restaurants in all Africa," the lady volunteered, "were in Senegal, but some of the most interesting foods were in Ethiopia, in Addis Ababa."

"And wherever we went, after the women taught me what they knew, I gave them lessons in cooking," Mrs. Sandler said. "I'm a born teacher. I showed them how to handle a French knife and how to handle the swivel cutter. I even showed them how to handle a coconut. They were doing it in the long, tedious way before that (with a spear-shaped cutter). Isn't that wild? I showed them how to heat the coconut in the oven and then with a hammer, crack, crack, crack. And then to pare away the rind with the cutter. They were absolutely thrilled."

Mrs. Sandler has more nerve than the law should allow.

I went around talking to folks in service. Everyone I talked to agreed that "service" jobs were excellent for gathering information on the life style of W.F.'s. Most of the people in "service" that I talked to had lots to say about W.F.'s. Lot of things are generalities, but there is a lot of validity to these generalities. I mean, when you be living with people for close to 400 years, nursing their children, washing their underwear, bed sheets, etc., and cooking their food, you form general impressions! Of course, you can't judge all W.F.'s from one family.

"White folks don't raise their children with no kind of manners. Slaps their hands when they should be cutting their asses. That brat I take care of is the most selfishest white bastard I ever took care of. Everytime I don't let him have his way, he scream I'm gonna tell my daddy and he'll fire you cause you a nigger and niggers are supposed to do what white people tell them. Also, I'm old enough to be his grandmother, and they allow him to call me by my first name. Now you tell me who taught that boy that—he must have overheard it from his parents. He sure didn't hear it from me. No. I'm telling you, white folks does not raise their children to respect other peoples.

You know another thing that the boy say to me? Ask me if when I takes a bath does my color wash off. I looked at that little sucker and I started to raise my dress and show him, but I just smiled and said, son, I was born black and will die black, and aint no detergent or white tornado or Mr. Clean can wash it off."

> Sixty years in these folks' world
> The child I work for calls me girl
> I say "yes ma'am" for working sake.[1]
> —Maya Angelou

It is rather traditional for little Sally to call the maid by her first name. Beulah can be any age and it's Beulah. Nothing depresses me more than to see a woman who could be my grandmother on a first name basis with some snotty-nose kid.

Out of the mouths of babes we hear and learn a lot about what Charles and Anne think of Beulah and her people.

"My Grandmother worked for a judge in Mobile, Alabama. He was known for being kind to nigras. Kind of a liberal cracker. Anyhow, Grandmama says she was serving the dinner to the family and they were talking about old Frank who had died that day and the little child yelled out, 'Mommy, Mommy, did the nigger die with his hat on?' The judge shushed the child up, made him leave the table and said to my Grandmother, 'Carrie, I'm sorry about that. I always taught him to say Darkey.'"

[1] Maya Angelou, *Just Give Me a Cool Drink of Water 'Fore I Die*. New York: Random House, 1971, p. 25. © 1969 by Hirt Music Inc. Printed by permission.

My friend Sister Amanda, who lives in Chicago and has worked all her life in "service," says that the children ask you the damnedest things. Sister Amanda is light-skinned, but not light enough to pass. She says that the silliest thing she remembers is when the kid said,

"Amanda," [again calling by her first name] "are you German?"
"No."
"Do you speak German?"
"No."
"What are you?"
"I am colored."
"Oh, then you speak colored."

Miss Maud Shaw's book, *White House Nanny*, has an interesting paragraph in regard to children asking questions about color:

One remarkable thing about children is the complete un-awareness of any difference between themselves and coloured people. The Kennedys used to have a coloured manservant up at Hyannis Port named George. George was a great favourite of Caroline's in her toddler days, and he had a remarkable gift of patience with the little girl. She used to talk to him for hours on end about absolutely nothing at all, just babbling on happily while George listened and nodded and said "yes" and "no" in all the right places. . . .

Anyway, Caroline never once remarked about his colour until one time when we were all down at Palm Beach. Caroline noticed for the first time that she was turning brown in the hot sunshine, and then she discovered for herself that George was permanently coloured.

"George," she said to him. "How did you get that colour? I've been in the sun all day and I'm only a bit brown."

"Well, miss," chuckled George, "I've been lying in the sun all my life, I guess."

After that she never asked another question about the subject.[2]

We would hope she was given many answers.

[2] Maud Shaw, *White House Nanny*. London: Frewin, 1968.

A big complaint is that the W.F.'s have the nerve of blaming the bad habits of their children on the maids. A sister I know who works in Flushing, New York, told me that the mother was always telling her to let the child be free to express himself. "The little brat was embarrassing and I just let him go on continuing to make a white ass out of himself. Didn't his Mama say let him express himself? Well, I did and this went on and on. Mind you now she knew all about it but don't you know that one day she had some important (at least she say they were important) company in her house and the kid showed out so bad, even she was embarrassed. And would you believe who she said was at fault—ME!"

I think it is a damn shame that after all we have done for white folks, they blame the bad habits their children got on us!

Another thing that most of the sisters that I talked to complained about was that they were always accused of stealing anything that was EVER missing. Whether it was lost, chewed up by the dog, misplaced by the children, ripped off by their friends, or legitimately stolen by a burglar—a lot of innocent sisters were fired from their jobs.

I remember as a child a case of a maid in Philadelphia who lost her job and her life. They said she stole jewelry from her employer and then murdered her. Corrine Skyes, the accused, was twenty years old when she died in the electric chair.

This is a story that a sister who had worked seven years for a Mr. & Mrs. Robert Dillon Overboard of Westchester told me.

"Off and on during the whole time I worked for the Overboards, Mrs. had ccused me, but it didn't mount to much because the things were always found befoe I could quit. I wasn't bout to let her fire me. Sometime when she would get real ugly and just bout ready to fire me I would say, 'Mrs. Overboard, you is going too far out to sea now, and if you thinks I stole something from you I will quit cause I don't want to work where I aint trusted.' Then she would say, 'Now Lillie Mae, let us search the house again. You've been with us for so long it would be a black spot on your reference for me to have to fire you over a misunderstanding.' And that was nother thing, she always called me Lillie Mae and my name is Peaches. Lillie Mae was the woman who worked for her before me. Lillie Mae left her to go back home to Birmingham, Alabama.

"Anyhow, one day Mrs. Overboard was screaming, 'Where the hell is my dunhill!' I told her I didn't know him. She llowed 'I mean a solid gold cigarette lighter, fool.' And that's when I said enough is enough. 'First off, you calls me out my name, and then you ccuse me of taking your "dunhill"—Now, I don't know who or what "dunhill" is—If it's a man, I wants you to know I don't truck with no white men. And if it's a cigarette lighter like you say, I don't smoke no cigarettes. This is not the first time you is ccuse me of stealing. But I bet you it will be the last. And I would suggest you ask your son where the hell your precious dunhill is. The way that boy has been acting is just how my sister's boy act, and he be on dope. And my sister lives with me, so I ought to know a junkie when I sees one. I always did think it funny that he was so willing to drive me home. I couldn't figure out why the hell a white boy want to be hanging out in Harlem after dark at times like this. Bet you your Mr. Dunhill is in a bar on Lenox Avenue and your son is in the land of nod. I'm as sure of that as I am that my ass is Black! So you, your bald-headed, pot-bellied husband, your hippie daughter, and your junkie son can all jump.'"

Working for W.F.'s is something all Black people know something about. Maybe aint nobody in your family working for them now but they used to.

I talked to a sister who grew up in Brooklyn in a middle-class family. But just cause her mama wasn't a domestic don't mean she don't feel about it—like Don L. Lee say, "I never wrote a love letter but that doesn't mean I don't love."[3] She said to me:

"I'll never forget the period of my life when we lived in Flat-bush. We moved there from Bedford-Stuyvesant, and I was still going to school at the time. Well, there's a transfer station on the subway, I think it's Franklin Avenue, where everybody who's going from Bedford-Stuyvesant to Flatbush has to wait for the

[3] Don L. Lee, *Don't Cry, Scream.* Detroit: Broadside Press, 1969. Reprinted by permission of Broadside Press.

train. It's an outdoor subway station. But the thing was, here I stood on the Franklin Ave. Station platform going the other way. I had to stand there, books in my arms, sun coming into my eyes, and it was early in the morning and I felt sleepy and vulnerable. And there were all my people on the other side. Nothing but Black folks, Black women, going on out to Flatbush. I don't know, there was more to it than sadness in what I felt as I looked at them all. There was just a feeling of the enormity and uniformity of it as a social fact. And then it wasn't 'them all' over there, it was 'us all.' "

One of my cousins who is a "retired" domestic lives in Washington and has a house full of furniture and appliances, plus an air conditioner, stereo, etc. I asked her why she had so many things. She said cause she had spent years working in white people's homes and she knew what a home was supposed to look like. She wanted to have what they had. She said everytime the madame would buy something, she'd buy the same at a thrift store. She said most of the stuff she never used, but she had it and so "White folks aint no better than I am cause I got just what they got."

Black people have a certain sophistication about "good taste," etc. They can tell which W.F.'s is which. This same cousin with the air conditioner which is never turned on, told me that once when she was in Cape Cod, she was on the beach and she told her missus, "My, that lady is a millionaire, aint she?" Her missus asked her how she knew, and she said she could tell. "You gets to know the real McCoy from the Ginsbergs, and you can smell new money a mile away." The lady in question was Mrs. Butterick. I asked her how she knew, and she said cause the lady was plain and she had on a custom-made one-piece bathing suit.

She told a story once of working in a house for some nouveau riche W.F.'s and having to leave cause their furniture and stuff was in bad taste. She said that they had never heard of Louis Vuitton and used Samsonite luggage. She said they used Corning Ware pots and had no real China at all. I asked her how she knew that they were nouveau riche and not economy-minded. She said because she was talking to the madame one day and mentioned the tureen in her breakfront cabinet, and the madame asked "What's that?" She said any white person what aint got a grandmother who has a breakfront cabinet with a tureen in it is nouveau riche.

This same cousin also told me of a party she served and how she could tell the old rich W.F.'s from the new ones. She said there was an expression that white people who come into money (one way or another) used to say, "Thank God, now I can live like W.F.'s." Just as she said it, I remembered a few years ago on 2nd Avenue I saw a white actor I knew, and we exchanged the usual, Hey, How you do's, and are you working. He'd gotten a job on a soap opera and he and his family had moved into a six-room apartment. He said, "Thank God, now we can live like white people." I remember that I understood what he meant, but I looked at him strange cause I couldn't understand how he could say that to me. He had no such thoughts. Just shook my hand and walked away, whistling about his good fortune.

Back to the party. She said she watched some of the white people wait to eat until others did, because they didn't know which fork to use. Some, she said, wouldn't take certain things off the tray of hors d'oeuvres cause she was sure they didn't know what they were. The conversations at the party, she said, were hardly party type stuff. She said if Black people had been at that party they would have put some life in it. Most of it, according to her, was about who was wearing the wrong dress, who had a toupee, whose husband's stomach was the biggest, etc.

She talked a lot about how different W.F.'s on different socio-economic levels dress their children. She said the richest ones, whose children go to private schools, put dungarees and Frances Esner polo shirts on, and there's the up-and-comers who put Orbach's import shop togs on theirs.

> "The richer they are, the longer the hair. You go to any elementary school in a white middle-class neighborhood and the children got crew cuts—around 90th Street and Madison Avenue, all you see is hair blowing in the wind."

One of the biggest complaints was the amount of work expected to be done in service.

"My name is Selma Macon and I am from Savannah, Ga. I have ten brothers and seven sisters. I worked for a long time for Mr. and Mrs. Beauregard Campbell Dull Pickens. I was a mother's helper and did light housekeeping, ironing, cleaning and once a week I would wash the windows in the basement, every other month I would wax the parkay floors in the main ballroom, and do all the hand laundry and all the children's things and all Mr. Beau's shirts and all Mrs. Pickens' stockings and underwear.

"I also cooked the breakfast for the children, and brunch for Mrs. Pickens and hot lunch for the little ones in the nursery group and sort of an afternoon snack for Mr. Beau and an after-school-pick-me-up for the older children and then around 5:00, I would make things for high tea or hors d'oeuvres, if they were having a cocktail party. I cooked dinner for the kids around 6:30 and supper for Mr. and Mrs. around nine. If they had more than eight in for dinner, the head cook would handle it.

"Around eleven, I would prepare sandwiches or some kind of snack in case they wanted something in the middle of the night. Finally they moved to California. Mrs. Beauregard said, as soon as they got settled, they would send for me. After about three months, I got an envelope with the bus fare, I guess'd it was them since I didn't know anybody besides them in California, but I didn't go. I kept the money."

I heard stories wherever I went.

One day I was in a department store and a young girl stopped me and asked me what size did I think a little girl about the size of Chandra (my daughter who was with me) wore—I told her and we talked some—I found out she was Haitian and a domestic here. I invited her to come home with me and have some coffee. I explained that I was doing a book and that I would like to hear some of her experiences, both in Haiti and here. She told me that she was married and had two Chandras (children) and that they and her husband were still in Haiti. She had been working, sleep-in, for a family in New Jersey, trying to save enough money to bring them here.

She had recently quit the family in New Jersey because the young boy of the house (22, she was 20) kept trying to get next to her—she finally told the father, who said: "Maybe if you wore less suggestive clothes, my son wouldn't be tempted."

After the family in N.J., she worked for a well-known white painter, but that didn't work out either. She said he was too weird and that his friends were weirder. They would all be pawing on her and telling her how "fantastic" her color was, what a "gas it would be to paint her nude," etc.—she quit.

Service jobs are not confined to milady's house.

I talked to a woman who worked in a fancy "French Dry Cleaning" place on Madison Avenue where she was sort of "The Girl" (Sweeping floors, wiping counters, picking up hangers, etc.) She said her husband was the delivery man for the cleaners and their customers used to tip him a quarter, no matter how much extra trouble, no matter how many clothes he'd bring. A straight 25¢, if anything! One day she said she was so angry at her husband getting quarters, she liberated a dress. She said she felt it was due her owing to the small salary she and her husband got. She said: "I got tired of seeing them bitches bring in dresses that weren't even dirty and cost more than two weeks of my salary. Plus they would fuss about the $2.00 cleaning cost. So when I needed a dress for the Liberation Ball in Baltimore last Spring, I 'liberated' me a dress."

Reminds me of the sister who told me that her mother was a laundress in Baltimore and her mother had worked out a system where she (the daughter) wore the clothes. That is her mother would work a week behind so that her child could wear the clothes of the young mistress to school.

I talked to a lady who worked in a beauty salon. She cleaned up the salon after closing and waited on the W.F.'s while the place was open. When I asked her about her job she had this comment:

"It wasn't really hard work but the smell was terrible, their hair smelled funny when it was wet. Funny thing when I first started working there, I was fresh from Savannah, Ga., and didn't know nothing from nothing. I lived to find out they used as many hair straighteners, sprays, greases, rinsers, etc., as colored people."

Another friend of mine told me about a friend of her's who worked for years in a famous Hollywood nightclub as a "ladies room attendant."

The stories she told can't be told here for fear of libel suits from the movie stars involved. But let me clue you in on this, remember in the movies how the dude always gave the dame "some change for the ladies room"; they should have filmed the happenings of the ladies room. Anyhow my friend told me (the parts she could tell), that there was one observation that struck her,

> "White women are afraid of getting old. They are very vain, very competitive, much more competitive toward each other than sisters are to one another. They think they are the most beautiful women in the world and that any other women are 'exotic freaks.' But them white women are the ones. One old movie star used to keep a jar of wrinkle cream in the club and every time she came to the ladies room she would touch up the wrinkles. The cream cost $35.00 a jar and she never gave me more than a quarter tip. There are other things that went on in the ladies room, but they wasn't too lady like so I'm not gonna tell."

Many well known persons started their careers in domestic service. Some became famous as cooks, domestics, spies, hair culturists, literary geniuses. Zora Neale Hurston at one time was working as a domestic and as she was cleaning, her employer was lounging and reading an article written by Zora. John A. Williams once worked as a butler. Addison Gayle was a sleeping car porter. Chester Himes was an elevator operator.

A well known poetess that I know told me that she once had a job as a domestic in Indiana. She said the lady hired her for the day and saved all the week's work for that day!!

> "I had to do everything in one day: floors, windows, ironing, washing and waxing of the floors, plus all the dishes. This woman was so lazy that if she ran out of clean dishes to use, rather than wash, she would use paper plates. One day, I was tired and really fed up with her ways; so I decided to 'sabotage' the whole day. First off I threw out all the vacuum cleaner bags and put a hole in the one that was left in the vacuum machine . . . I sprayed paint 'by mistake' instead of cleaner on the win-

dows. I did a lot of other things that day, cause I didn't care what she thought of me. I was determined to quit that day anyhow. But the best thing that happened, was when I was cleaning her bedroom and she was fussing about how she wanted underneath the bed cleaned and I pretended that I just couldn't understand; so she got on her knees and cleaned underneath and said: 'that's how I want it done.' I smiled cause it was already done . . . by her."

Another who worked in service was Susie King Taylor. She was a laundress, and became a spy, a nurse and teacher. During the War Between the States, some say she had a way of hanging out clothes to send messages to the Union Army.

Another spy who was heavy in espionage work was Mary Elizabeth Bowser.

Mary Elizabeth Bowser of Richmond, Virginia. Prior to the War (Civil), this young former slave had been sent to Philadelphia for schooling by her employer, Elizabeth Van Lew. After the War began, Mary Elizabeth was called back home to assist Miss Van Lew in espionage work.

Elizabeth Van Lew became the leader of the Union supporters in Richmond, engaged in activities which greatly aided Generals Grant and Butler. When Elizabeth Bowser returned to Richmond, she was placed in the Confederate White House as a servant of Jefferson Davis. While dusting furniture, Elizabeth, who pretended illiteracy, read dispatches and orders, then passed the information on to Miss Van Lew through another spy, who went to the Van Lew plantation daily to secure eggs and other farm produce. Often while serving dinner to the Confederate President, Elizabeth Bowser was able to overhear information involving troop movements and other pertinent plans of the army. This information was relayed to Miss Van Lew, who then passed it on to General Grant.

Though her daily espionage activities placed her in a most precarious position, Elizabeth Bowser served undetected throughout the War as a Union spy in the Confederate White House.[4]

[4] Charles H. Wesley and Patricia W. Romero, *Negro Americans in the Civil War—From Slavery to Citizenship.* Washington: United Publishing, 1967.

A former laundress who became a mahogany millionairess was Sarah Jane Walker, later to be called Madame Walker of the hair grease fame. Indeed, it is said that after working for years as a laundress, and seeing what a hot comb could do to wrinkled clothes, she surmised what a hot comb could do to crinkled hair. It did it so well, that when she died at the age of 50, she left an estate of two million dollars.

At about the same time Madame Walker was tearing down old brownstone buildings and building a $90,000 castle of Indiana limestone on lots 108–110 in West 136th Street in Harlem, Sister Pig Foot Mary came on the scene. Pig Foot Mary, "a huge Amazon,"⁵ whose real name was Lillian Harris, rented a tiny booth at Lenox Avenue and 135th Street and sold pigs feet, hog maws, chitterlins and corn on the cob. Lillian was from Mississippi and could not read or write. She had run away in the fall of 1901 and come to New York. Penniless, "within a week after her arrival she had earned five dollars as a domestic."⁶ With half the money she bought pigs feet, and with the other half she bought a washtub. When she died, she not only owned the stand she worked from on Lenox Avenue, she owned lots of real estate and left a considerable bundle of money.

Let's not forget that Harriet Tubman rocked many a cradle before taking the liberty line. Sojourner Truth was a mammy for her Dutch master's children.

The most illustrious mammy of all must certainly be Mammy Pleasant. Mary Ellen Pleasant, who became known as "Mammy Pleasant," was born around 1814 in Philadelphia of Black and Indian parentage. Some say she was born free, some say she was given her freedom later. Mammy Pleasant was a friend of John Brown, and was said to have helped finance the raid at Harper's Ferry. She was also a famous cook and housekeeper in San Francisco.

Herbert Asbury, telling of the great trouble in getting servants in San Francisco during the California gold rush, and the airs that most domestics had put on, says, "A notable exception to this foolery was Mammy Pleasant, a gigantic Negress from New Orleans, black as the inside of a coal-pit, but with no Negroid features whatever, whose culinary exploits were famous. She said flatly that she was a cook, and would be called nothing else. She

---

⁵ Roi Ottley and William J. Weatherby, eds., *The Negro in New York: An Informal Social History, 1626–1940.* New York: Praeger, 1969, p. 187.
⁶ Ibid.

arrived in the early part of 1850, preceded by her reputation, and was besieged by a crowd of men, all anxious to employ her, before she had so much as left the wharf at which her ship had docked. She finally sold her services at auction for five hundred dollars a month, with the stipulation that she would do no washing, not even dish-washing. This was the highest wage paid to a cook, although several others received as high as three hundred dollars a month."[7]

Some of the most often said generalities about W.F.'s as employers were:

"They lazy."

"They Dirty."

"They eat funny."

"They don't half raise their children."

"They Cheap."

"Now I work for a lady who got more money than Carter got liver pills, but she is the cheapest thing what God ever created when it come to food. Listen to this. She on East 57th Street. Goes to Vermont in winter. Got a house on Fire Island in the summer. Got a husband and three children. She got a mink coat and a red fox maxi coat, buys her dresses on Madison Avenue where the dresses starts at $300. I know how much, cause they sends me to pick them up. She has to have everything altered, cause one of her hips is higher than the other and they fixes her dresses so you can't tell it. She buys them brats of hers imported everything, even underwear. Look on they drawers, be a tab on there says Swissland. With all this, she eats like they po white trash. I don't eat with them myself. I goes out to lunch. Last summer when I was still sleepin'-in we was getting ready to go to Fire Island for the weekend. I fixed a pot roast that Friday night for dinner. She said take what was left with us to Fire Island. So Saturday night on Fire Island we had more pot roast. Sunday we had pot roast sandwiches and, would you believe, back in New York for Monday night supper that hussy put the rest of the pot roast—which weren't no bigger than a baby's

[7] J. A. Rogers, *Sex and Race, Vol. III.* Privately published: New York, 1944, pp. 311–12.

fist—in her blender with celery and onions and mayonnaise and served it on lettuce. Called it Pot Roast Dressing. Honey, I took the A train home and ate me some fried chicken, rice, and collard greens."

I hate to demistify the myth that we loved working for them but the following stories are true. All over the planet the desire to leave massa's service was never far from Beulah, Delcie, Lillie Mae or Sophie's mind.

Today is Saturday. The whites in Dangan usually spend their Saturdays at the European Club which is run by M. Jenopoulos. All the houseboys are free at twelve.

On my way back to the location I met Sophie, the African mistress of the agricultural engineer. She seemed angry about something.

"What's wrong with a day off?" I asked her.

"I am a proper fool," she said. "The one day my white man leaves the keys of his strongbox in his trouser pocket during siesta is the day I don't go through them."

"You want to stop him going back to his own country?"

"Fuck his country and fuck him. It makes me sick when I think of all the time I've been going with the uncircumcised sod and what have I made out of it? Now today comes my real chance and I miss it . . . I must have mud between my ears stead of brains . . ."

"Ah, don't you love your white man? He's the most handsome white man in Dangan you know."

She looked at me for a moment and retorted.

"You talk as if you weren't black. You know very well, whites haven't got what we can fall in love with . . ."

"So?"

"So what? I'm waiting . . . waiting my chance; and then Sophie is off to Spanish Guinea . . . Well, what do you expect? We don't mean anything to them either. It's a good job it's mutual. Only I'm sick and tired of hearing 'Sophie, don't come today. I've got a European coming to see me at the house,' 'Sophie, you can come, the European has gone,' 'Sophie, when you see me with a white lady don't look at me, don't greet me' and all the rest."

We walked on side by side without speaking, thinking our own thoughts.

"What a fool I am," she said again as she went off.[8]

One sister who was a maid to a rather liberal, rich white family on Philadelphia's mainline ran this story down to me.

"Well, in a way you could say I was attached to them. I mean I worked for them for twenty-five years. But they wasn't like *my* family. They had two boys and one girl. All of them grew up to be hippies. The girl lives in New York in the East Village with a nigger, and I think both of the boys is on dope. They went to good schools. They went to college out here on the mainline. You know the one out here where when the black students went to call on the man he had a heart attack.

"Mrs. Howell wasn't mean or nothing, but still I didn't like her. I couldn't understand how come she dressed and looked so plain, always wearing funny looking clothes. She had midi's way before they came back in style this year. Wore a bunch of funny looking skirts she said was from Guatemala. With all the money she had, you'd thought she would shop at Nan Duskin's or someplace like that. They house didn't have no sitting furniture, either—a bunch of skinny chairs a friend of hers made, no curtains at the windows; used to make me bust my back keeping them windows clean, too. And what they ate. Girl, it wasn't to be believed. I got so sick of cream cheese and jelly sandwiches. I used to feel like date nut bread. I got to admit I didn't work too hard, physically. Mrs. Howell was so self-conscious and was so upset about the way Negroes were treated that she never asked me to do the real heavy work. She would do it herself, and he would wash and wax the floors. They didn't have a rug in the joint. They had a few handmade Mexican ones on the wall.

"Everytime something was in the paper about Negroes being treated bad, Mrs. Howell would ask me if I wanted to go visit my family in Baltimore. I'd always say yes, and she would have the chauffeur drive me down. My family would laugh and laugh

[8] Ferdinand Oyono, *Houseboy*. New York: Collier Books, 1970, p. 92.

to see me come driving up our street in a long black car with a white chauffeur.

"Mrs. Howell gave me all her clothes, but I'd give them to the goodwill cause they wasn't nothing like what I wanted to wear. When I started working for her my daughter was small and I kept her with me. Then when school time came, she went to live with my family in Baltimore. Sometimes she would spend summers with us, at their summer place in New Jersey, but still I missed her growing up with me. I knew Mrs. Howell's children better than my daughter. When my daughter finished school and got married with babies of her own, I figured it was time for me to quit Mrs. Howell and her family and take care of mine. I did, and never regretted or missed having the $50.00 a week. After all, blood's thicker than water."

One thing that kept coming back when I talked to people who worked in service was that W.F.'s will ask us to do things they wouldn't let their own kin do.

"They is shameless around their servants. This woman I worked for well when her boyfriend come over, she just kiss him and hug all up like I was a piece of her bad-taste furniture but the worst thing is everytime she get her period—she leaves her things all over the place and expects me to clean it up. The shameless hussy."

I recently read a similar rap.

Baklu with his right hand up to his nose was holding one of Madame's sanitary towels between the thumb and finger of his left. He tried to come into the kitchen. The cook shut the door against him and began to swear. Baklu went back to the wash-house, roaring with laughter. He came back a few moments later sniffing his fingers which were dripping with water and trying to dry them by waving them about in the air.

The cook half opened the door and shouted through, "Don't come in here, don't come in here."

"What's the matter?" said Baklu, laughing. "You're getting very particular. Just to look turns you over. What about me, I have to wash it with my hands."

He shook his hands about and went on:

"What do you expect. Everyone has his job. You're in the pots and pans and I'm in the washtub."

The cook watched him, horrified. Baklu still went on.

"What amazes me is that you still haven't got over these things," he said to the cook. "It can't be the first time you've seen one of them . . ."

The cook passed his hand over his face. "It's not the same, seeing them," he said, "the eye seems to be a long way away. What would our ancestors say if they saw us washing things like that for the whites?"

"There are two worlds," said Baklu, "ours is a world of respect and mystery and magic. Their world brings everything into the daylight, even the things that weren't meant to be . . . Well we must get used to it . . . We laundrymen are like doctors, we touch the things that disgust ordinary men."

"What are we to these white?" asked the cook. "Everyone I have ever worked for has handed over these things to the laundryman as if he wasn't a man at all . . . these women have no shame . . ."

"Shame, you talk about . . ." burst out Baklu. "They are corpses. Do corpses feel shame? How can you talk about shame for these white women who let themselves be kissed on the mouth in full daylight in front of everybody? Who spend all their time rubbing their heads against their husbands' cheeks or their lovers' more often, sighing, not caring where they are? Who are only good in bed and can't even wash their pants or their sanitary towels . . . They say they work hard in their own country. But those who come here . . ."

Baklu was going on with this when Madame appeared on the veranda. He looked at her, gave a little nod, and winked at us.

"Washman," she called, "what are you doing over there?"

"Nothing, Madame, I was just talking about my girlfriend . . ."

Madame bit her lip so as not to laugh. She forced herself to say, "Back to work. This is not the time . . ."

Baklu hurried off towards the washhouse.[9]

---

[9] Ibid., pp. 95–96.

Everybody knows the Pullman Porter. "From the time the Pull-man Company began its operation in 1867 the porters' work has been practically a Negro monopoly."[10]

That thing about the porter always being Black, and the conductor being white on trains used to really disturb me when I was a child. (Same thing in the poultry market and grocery store in my neighborhood.) White man takes the money, Black man does the work. White man does the head job, Black man does the menial job. As I got older I would try to give my ticket or money to the porter. In my naïveté, I thought that perhaps he would/could "stand up like a man" and take it. But the porter always smiled, said "thank you, the conductor will take care of you."

All our South Carolina/Philadelphia train trips were in coach, and so I don't really know what it is like to have ever personally "had" a Pullman porter. I have heard from the porters, their families, and others what it's like. It makes me smile as I remember going back and forth down South and how much I used to envy the families of Pullman porters because they had passes instead of tickets.

I have read much about A. Philip Randolph and how he tightened that whole thing up. In 1925, when Randolph was trying to organize the Brotherhood of Sleeping Car Porters and Maids, he met much hostility and resistance.

> The Pullman Company absolutely refused to have anything to do with the new Brotherhood and proceeded to fight it with every weapon at its command . . . At Pittsburgh the superintendent openly declared that he would fire any man who joined the organization, while at St. Louis, the porters were told that if they were fools enough to join the union their places would be taken by Mexicans and Japanese.
> . . . The new organization was represented as "subversive," "Socialistic," "Communistic," and "Red."[11]

The company gave the brotherhood a hard time and ignored the union. They used very "repressive tactics." They disregarded the civil and seniority rights of porters belonging to the brotherhood. "The placing of Filipinos on club cars in violation of seniority

[10] Sterling D. Spero and Abram L. Harris, *The Black Worker*, New York, Antheneum, 1969, p. 434.
[11] Ibid., p. 437.

rights"[12] was just one way to invalidate the guarantees given the employees under the brotherhood plan.

Sometimes the company was not so subtle and "actually permitted the discharge of a number of employees for organization activity without making any attempt to disguise its motives."[13]

In spite of this, the brotherhood grew, and in the fall of 1927 had 7,300 members out of 12,000 porters in the service.

I remember when we would get the train in Philadelphia, either the Palmland or the Southland. There was another called the Silver Meteor but it was too expensive, at least that is what my mother told me. (Mama said they only had Pullman seats.) We would usually leave on Friday night. The train left the same time every night, 10:57, and we'd arrive around 1 P.M. in Fairfax. We took shoe box lunches full of fried chicken, light bread, pound cake. My earlier memories are getting on in Philadelphia and changing in Washington, D.C., to the Jim Crow train. It was awful. We'd get on in Philadelphia and sit down anywhere there was a seat. There were always many more Black than white getting on, but rarely would there not be a white.

In Washington, I remember, it was a moving black sea of cardboard boxes, cheap sweaters, crying babies, and sleepy children loading up the "Jim Crow" cars. When we finally settled down again I was usually asleep, before we even left Washington.

During the night I'd wake up and eat, drink pop, and maybe make some friends. We always made friends on our trips. Seems like we'd always find *someone* who was getting off round Fairfax or Estill. Mama even found some of our cousins she hadn't seen for years. After dawn, most folks would wake up and eat breakfast (from the shoe boxes). Sometimes the porter would come along with hot coffee from the dining car, but this usually happened around Raleigh, N.C., when they put the breakfast car on.

Sometimes, if it was a long enough stop, we would get off and buy coffee from inside the station. Mostly we did without and drank canned juices and pop. We would carry those picnic things with ice so we always had a cold drink. Around about Columbia I remember a porter named Mr. Sam who would come around selling ice cold watermelon. We always bought some, and Mama would always say,

[12] Ibid., p. 444.
[13] Ibid., p. 445.

"tastes good but don't taste good as Bubba and Bill's watermelons."
Then, soon as the train would pull out of Columbia, she'd say,
"Well, it won't be as long now as it has been," and we would wash
up, fix our hair, and change clothes for getting off the train in
Fairfax.

All the times (and there were many, many) I rode as a child to
South Carolina/Pennsylvania, I never ate in the dining car. I'd been
in there to "take out coffee," but never to sit down and eat. I'd always heard they didn't allow colored in the dining car.

When I grew up and rode the train, the dining car was a mystery
to me. First time I ate in there I was nervous as hell, although I tried
to appear blasé. I had my children with me and we went for breakfast. I was literally shaking. I imagined that everyone could tell it was
my first time and could see that I was making all kinds of mistakes.

First thing that threw me off was when the waiter told me to
write down my order. I asked how come I couldn't tell him. Did
he think I was too inarticulate to pronounce the menu? He assured
me that everyone does that. Then I wanted to know why the company made the customer write the order. Was that because they
thought that the waiters were too dumb and couldn't write, remember orders, etc.? He told me he had no idea why the railroad did
what they did, but that they must have a good reason. I asked him if
he accepted everything that W.F.'s did as good reason. He asked me
did I want to eat or talk politics. I forget what we ordered, but it was
unattractive, bland, and expensive.

After that I went back to box lunches on the train. Sometimes,
if the trip is long, I go to the dining car and have coffee or tea, or
maybe have a small snack, but not for no serious eating.

My cousin Minnie's husband used to be a sleeping car porter, and
he told me that he'd have a hard time tearing the white ladies out
their husband's arms on the platform, and next morning it would
take him and a red cap to pry Miss Anne out of the arms of some
dude she'd meet in the Pullman.

And think of the stories coming out of hotels. If only the walls
could rap, we'd find out how that poor girl Zsa Zsa got in this mess:

The room in the Dayton was supposed to have been vacant.
So it was assigned to Zsa Zsa Gabor, in town for a summer-
theater production. But when Zsa Zsa walked in and switched on
the lights, she discovered that the room was occupied by a couple

of stark-naked men. "I was petrified," she said. "It was scary."
The outraged Zsa Zsa checked into a rival hotel and refused to
be mollified when the manager of the first hotel had the message
"Zsa Zsa, We Love You" emblazoned on his marquee and sent
her a bouquet. "He's worse than an ex-husband," said she. "He
sent me white mums, which are for dead people."[14]

Walls can't talk, but chambermaids can. I asked a friend of mine
who was a chambermaid in a midtown Philadelphia hotel to run it
down:

"Well, first off, they act like I ain't a person. They say and do
anything in front of me. I hates to go to work everyday. White
folks is so shocking. One time I knocked on a room door and
nobody answered, so I figured it weren't nobody there. So I
went on in and there was the two mens what rented the room,
all hugged up together on the floor, not on the bed, but, Child,
they was on the floor. Well, I turned to go out and they says,
'You can make the bed if you want. We're finished with it.'
Child, you could have knocked me over with a hat feather. I
hadn't never heard or seen nothing like that kind of foolish-
ness in my life.

"Another time, I walked in on a couple who was sitting round
their room naked as they came into the world. I told em, I'd
come to clean the room. They said they didn't mind, and I said
I mined and I wouldn't clean the room lessen they cover up
their bodies.

"Child, I have seen all kinds of things, working in hotels. I
don't like my job, but I am not educated and it's all I know.
Folks think not being educated means not having no feelings.
I've got plenty feelings. I don't mind when people don't leave a
tip. It could matter less. But I do mind when they pass me in
the hall, or I be in the room, and they talk to me like I am a
slave or something less even. I hate to talk bad about them, but
they is nasty, girl. If you could see the sheets.

"I don't dislike white folks. I just don't understand them. They
got a different way from us. They eats different foods, and take
it from me, they smells different. You ever smell one when they
just washed their hair? You know, it's a funny thing; they say

we smell bad, but the Lord know, iffen you did the kind of work that we does, you is bound to smell, cause you is bound to sweat, and sweat will equal a strong odor. But they have another kind of smell, Child. Sometimes I don't wanna even go in the rooms. You know what makes me maddest with them is that they don't treat me like I am a human being, too. If they throw they clothes on the floor, I leave them there. What is that thing that queens and em have? Ladies-in-waiting? Well, I ain't none of them. The only thing I wait on is quitting time and my paycheck."

This is nothing new. Its been going on and on and on . . .

. . . A Negro girl who worked during the nineties in a hotel patronized by travelling salesmen and construction workers building Clemson College, complained that her job "meant constant battle against unwanted advances, a studied ignoring of impudent glances, insulting questions."[15]

Here's my favorite chambermaid story. The *Daily News*, January 22, 1971, headlined the story "Waldorf Flap Causes Caseworker Uprising." This is the opinion of a maid on the upper floors, when asked . . .

. . . about Mrs. Cleola Hainsworth and her four children, whose one-night stay at the Waldorf was paid for by the city's Welfare Department: "Isn't it something? I've been here for 20 years and nothing like this has never happened before," said the stout woman with just a hint of an Irish brogue. "Ooh, the other maids, they was mad," she said. "Why, well, you know, they don't want to have to work for anybody on relief."

Mrs. Hainsworth herself wasn't too impressed with the Waldorf. She said:

"it's nice enough, but I've stayed in others just as nice . . . At the Manhattan Beach, the maids came in at 7 A.M. to clean up. Here it's after noon . . . I don't even have a food allowance here. We can't eat in the hotel. The prices are silly."

[15] George Brown Tindall, *South Carolina Negroes 1877–1900*. Baton Rouge: Louisiana State University Press, 1966, p. 298.

Oh, if only Old Black Joe would write a book and tell it like it was.

One of my friends' father has been a chauffeur for many years in and around Pittsburgh. He worked for many of the wealthy people in the area (the Mellons, the Carnegies, the McDonnells, etc.). Once he drove his boss to Montreal, Canada, to see a specialist at a hospital there. As they were standing on the hospital steps talking, a Canadian came by and stopped and stared at my friend's father, who is 6'4". The Canadian said "Biggest damn Indian I ever saw." The American said, "That ain't no Indian—that's a nigger."

Ex-President L. B. Johnson's chauffeur figures in with a bit of a story. The chauffeur (Black) was asked to drive the family car and beagle back to Texas. After hesitating, he said, "you see, what I'm sayin is that a man's got enough trouble getting across the South on his own without having a dog along."

An older brother that I talked to told me this one.

"I work in a job you might not think of as a service position but it is. I'm a groom. We have no job security, no pensions, medical benefits, nothing. In 1969 we had a boycott at Aqueduct. We blocked the road for nine days. They were real mad about the boycott. Cause the grooms are almost all Black and Puerto Rican, they feel like we should feel lucky to get any kind of jobs. I like workin round horses. I get that from my daddy. He was a jockey. Made lots of money in the old days when colored was the onliest jockeys you would mostly see. Like anything else when it got to be about a whole lot of money white people moved colored out of it. That's why we is the grooms—aint no money in it.

"Isaac Murphy was a famous jockey what they called the 'Black Archer.' He won the Kentucky Derby three times. That nigger could ride."

An artist friend of mine remembered working in a hospital in the kitchen, washing pots, pans, vats, scrubbing floors, iceboxes, and serving food. He'd take the steam wagon to the wards—for $45.00 a week. He used to rip off steaks, lamb and pork chops, chickens, etc., from the icebox. He wasn't the only one. Even with eat-ins and rip offs, they had food to waste. He said that the meals were mostly terrible but he ate there because on his salary he couldn't afford to eat meat lessen it was one of the rip-off steaks. The doctors ate differently than the workers and the patients. They had a different menu. "They had better food, and if they had any left, we could eat it. Lots of cats preferred to work in Doctors' Dining Room cause it was less work and better food."

A fly Puerto Rican brother told me he had to quit his job as a delivery boy with this local supermarket on 14th Street cause the women from Stuyvesant Town were extremists. That is, they went from one extreme to the other—either they told him he couldn't come in with the groceries, or they would try to molest him once he got in. He said one lady used to always ask for her groceries to be delivered on a weekday, when her children were in school, and Mr. Charlie at work, and it was just before Juan's lunch. She would always say, "How about a steak? I got extra. A little wine?" Juan would always refuse. She got mad and asked the manager of the supermarket not to send him anymore, the implication being that he was fresh with her. Aint that a bitch?

A brother I met in Atlanta told me,

"When I was in college during the summer vacation, lots of black college students and teachers studying for Masters, etc., used to be waiters in the resorts around Atlantic City and Asbury Park. Man, they worked the shit out of me, plus the people were mean. "Hey, feller, get a move on." "Boy, do this, do that." Like no basic respect for us. White folks used to load me up like I was a mule. And if you dropped your tray, you were fired. Plus you had to pay for the order. And, Man, when I say they wanted service, they wanted you to wait on them like they was GODS. The white man has a god complex. Most of the waiters had more education than the people they would be serving."

Another friend of mine who is a fine young brother, a fine photographer, and a fine painter, told me when he was in art school he worked up on the hill for the family his mama cleaned and cooked for, cutting grass. He said he would work in the sun, cutting grass from early morning until damn near dinner time and he made almost little or no money. The family claimed that he was almost like a son to them and they weren't *really* hiring him.

He says, "But I was *really* cutting grass. And they would give me a slim lunch. Cottage cheese, a small can of dietetic peaches, a glass of skim milk, and a piece of Halvah. Man, I was working and wanted some food. I told my mama but she was too embarrassed to steal from the kitchen. I asked her to give me something from the refrigerator, anything. But she didn't."

WHEN IN ROME[16]

Mattie dear
the box is full
take
whatever you like
to eat
    (an egg
    or soup
    . . . there ain't no meat)
there's endive there
and
cottage cheese
    (whew! if I had some
    black-eyed peas . . .)
there's sardines
on the shelves
and such
but
don't
get my anchovies
they cost
too much!
    (me get the
    anchovies indeed!
    what she think, she got—
    a bird to feed?)
there's plenty in there
to fill you up.
    (yes'm. just the
    sight's
    enough!
    Hope I lives till I get
    home
    I'm tired of eatin'
    what they eats in Rome . . .)

[16] Mari Evans, *I Am a Black Woman*, copyright © 1970 by Mari Evans. New York, Morrow, 1970, pp. 56–57. Reprinted by permission.

A friend of mine who is a Black Christian Nationalist remembers that, "My grandmother was the first Black Revolutionary I ever knew. During the War, when everyone was prickin' those little red buttons on the plastic bag that changed the color of that lard-like stuff to make margarine—well, we didn't have that, cause my grandmother stole butter from the crackers. She did a number of other things like

> half doing the cleaning
> scorching clothes
> half cleanin the vegetables
> breakin the gall of the liver of the chicken."

This kind of domestic action is not new. Been going on since slavery. Oh yes we have taken care of massa and missy. Done everthing we could.

Nursed them thru sickness.

Many servants upon receiving instructions on how not to fan too hard, would fan the last breath right out of massa or missy. If they were told not to let massa sit up or walk around for too long, they made sure that massa walked or sat up tired til he was too weak to even tell on them. We nursed them to death.

"Yes, I was here in slavery. I will be 86 years old the 15th of August. My master had 47 slaves. We all lived right in the yard below the white people's house . . .

". . . Old mistress got sick and I would fan her with a brush, to keep the flies off her. I would hit her all in the face; sometimes I would make out I was sleep and beat her in the face. She was so sick she couldn't sleep much, and couldn't talk, and when old master come in the house she would try to tell him on me, but he thought she meant I would just go to sleep. Then he would tell me to go out in the yard and wake up. She couldn't tell him that I had been hitting her all in the face. I done that woman bad. She was so mean to me.

"Well, she died and all the slaves come in the house just a hollering and crying and holding their hands over their eyes, just hollering for all they could. Soon as they got outside of the house they would say, 'Old God damn son-of-a-bitch, she gone on down to hell.' "[17]

[17] Social Science Institute, Fisk University, *The Unwritten History of Slavery*. Washington: NCR Microcard Editions, 1968, p. 67.

White woman for marriage, mulatto woman for f_____,
Negro woman for work. . . .
—An old Brazilian saying

Many times, growing up, I've heard women say I aint gonna let my daughter work in no white man's kitchen. They knew what went on there and didn't want it happening to their own. The white man is notorious for debasing young Black girls who are in service. For that matter, Black women.

One cousin of mine who lives in a small town in Tennessee was a cook for a Mr. & Mrs. Brooks for over twenty years. My cousin lived in a little house in back of the big house. She had six children, all of whom were fathered by Mr. Brooks. Mr. Brooks never had any white children although he was married to three sisters in one white family. When my cousin passed Mr. Brooks on the street she was not allowed to speak. She was obliged to step aside for him. And he never acknowledged her. The mother fucker.

The problem of white men abusing Black women "in service" is not confined to the slavery period. I remember many stories from Black women who talked of how "the mister" of the house would bother them. My friend Carolyn told me that her mother used to work in the South for a rich white family as one of their maids. This particular night they were asked to stay and serve the party. Carolyn's mother said she had a funny feeling about the party and decided not to work. Next day she heard one of the maids had been raped by one of the male guests who got drunk and had to have a Black woman.

My cousin Zipporah once told me that when she lived in Georgia as a child she used to help her mother out occasionally. Her mother worked for some W.F.'s on the proverbial hill. One day, when she was about 13, her mother was ill and sent her to work the day in her place. Mid-afternoon she came home crying and told her mother the missus had gone out for the afternoon and the mister came home and tried to rape her. Zipporah said her mother's first words were, "Child, for God's sake, don't tell your father. You'll get him kilted." Aunt Sarah said, what could a poor Black man do legally or physically to a rich white man who had tried to molest his daughter? What could he do and get away with—alive? She didn't tell him.

In the North it was more the white insurance man than the white man in the big house. Most people we knew had an insurance man who came once a week for a dollar. The amount you were insured for was vague, but we knew it was enough to bury you.

The "insurance man" was infamous and notorious when it came to young girls. Most times the mama wasn't home. She was out doing days work, and he'd find the young girls alone. A friend of mine told me,

"Everytime the insurance man came he would ask me to let him feel my breast and put his hands under my dress, and he'd give me 50¢—half of our insurance premium."

Those insurances!—We were the most insuranced people in the world. But we didn't have no theft insurance, no fire insurance, liability, accident, etc.—our's was for death.

"In case you dead on me, the state won't have to bury you."
"At lease I'll have enough money to give you a decent funeral."

Most of the time the insurance was for $500.00. That was enough (at that time I was a child) for a layout in Philadelphia, shipping the body to S.C. and a proper funeral and burial there.

White men have some weird ideas about Black women. Young and old. I hate walking by a group of white teenagers. Those pickley-face sons of oppressors will say the crudest, nastiest things imaginable.

Blondes think they get it when they go by a group of construction workers; try being Black like me and walking by. A Black woman doesn't even have to walk by a group—individual white men will commit individual acts of insult to the Black woman.

One spring afternoon I had lunch with a first cousin of mine to celebrate her discharge from the mental hospital, and as we walked up Park Avenue South, on the corner of 31st Street, an unshaven white man came running up to us shouting, "How much? How much?" He reached in his pocket and grabbed a five dollar bill and kept asking, "Is this enough?" I got scared cause my cousin had a quick temper, didn't like white people, and wasn't too stable to begin with. I was trying to calm my cousin down and get her away, when the man started shouting, "Please give me some pussy. I need black pussy. Black pussy today. Please, please." Well, my cousin heard him and she went out to lunch. She hit him with her purse, pulled his hair, called his mama out her name, and went to a police box to call the cops. We were right in front of a restaurant where a lot of off-duty taxi drivers eat, and I liberated one of the taxis, pushed my cousin in and we left before the police came.

III

Mammy, Aunt Jemima & Uncle Ben, the Gold Dust twins and the rest of the family

W.F.'s like to see smiling, colored faces serving. Why else would they put that brother on the Cream of Wheat box? I know of a white family that eats Cream of Wheat every morning with the box in the middle of the table. The lady of the house says it brings good luck to look at a Black man first thing in the morning. And since she aint married to one and there are no Blacks in the neighborhood . . .

Speaking of the lady of the house, a friend of mine told me that during the thirties when the W.F.'s had hard times, climbers would hire a colored maid even though they couldn't afford it just to make sure that Miss Anne didn't have to answer the door herself and thus be mistaken for the maid. These days, Miss Anne is sister Anne. Having decided that the sisterhood is powerful, she and her sisters don't care who answers the door, cause they aint home nohow. They are out to lib and the children are in a day care center.

Now who do you think is staffing the day care center? While Ms. Anne is out solving the feminine mystique, who is cleaning the house?

Above all looms the figure of the Black Mammy, one of the most pitiful of the world's Christs. Whether drab and dirty drudge or dark and gentle lady she played her part in the uplift of the South. She was an embodied sorrow—an anomaly cruci- fied on the cross of her own neglected children for the sake of the children of masters who bought and sold her as they bought and sold cattle. Whatever she had of slovenliness or neatness of degradation or of education she surrendered it to those who lived to lynch her sons and ravish her daughters. From her great full breast walked forth governors and judges, ladies of wealth and fashion, merchants and scoundrels who lead the South. And the rest gave her memory the reverence of silence.[1]

Black women as mammies are an American institution. W.F.'s who never had one feel unAmerican and dream and pray for a Black mammy.

The old cracker prayed on, "Lord, Lord, dear Lord, since I did not have a nice old colored mammy in my childhood, give me one in heaven, Lord. My family were too poor to afford a black mammy for any of my father's eight children. I were mammy-less as a child. Give me a mammy in heaven, Lord. Also a nice old Nigress to polish my golden slippers and keep the dust off my wings. But, Lord, if there be educated Nigras in heaven, keep them out of my sight . . .[2]

Everybody knows how I love you, oh, how I love you Mammy. Everybody knows how yo baby love shortn'bred—But I wanna know how come Sister Anne will find fulfillment as the first woman executive at chit chitty bang bang corporation, and Beulah will find her personhood cleaning Anne's house for a "decent" salary? Who's gonna take care of Anne's kids after day care center? You don't really believe that Anne's gonna leave her kid in the day care center ten hours a day. The little brat might get a complex.

More than likely, he's already got a mammy complex. W.F.'s have spent lots of energy, hundreds of hours, and thousands of dollars to keep mammy alive—in real and reel life, literature, TV, radio and their minds. The mammy mystique is so strong, that they see a little of mammy in every Black woman who works for them.

"Fortunately, I had two great ample-bosomed Negro women from North Carolina to help me through all twenty years of raising kids. First Gladys Francis, and then Ruth Jackson. Both pos-

---

[1] W. E. B. Du Bois, *The Gift of Black Folk*. Chicago: Johnson Reprint, 1969.
[2] Langston Hughes, "Cracker Prayer," in *Simple's Uncle Sam*, New York: Hill & Wang, 1965, pp. 124–25.

sessed the love and affection of Mammy in *Gone With the Wind,*
and I paid them the wages of an NAACP organizer."[3]

The big ample bosom of Mammy is as American as apple pie.
Everybody wants to rest in the big, soft, warm haven of Mammy's
black bosom. Mammy—I love you. Oh Mammy.
Big tittied bitch.
Big legged mama.
"an ass so big it screams of power."[4]
The big bosomed, black mammy is the prototype of the pin-up girl.
Think I'm kidding? Check it out . . . mammy, Gibson Girl, Aunt
Jemima, Jayne Mansfield . . . all had one thing in common . . . a
heaven for white men's greedy heads.

Talking bout titties, in a stationery store on Lexington Avenue
in Fun City, I found a card with six plastic replicas of an African
woman that show the rise and fall of her titties. The card read thus
. . . "nifty at 15; spiffy at 20; sizzling at 25; perky at 30; declining at
35; and droopy at 40." They were called Zulu-Lulu stirrers and were
guaranteed "To make your guests bust out laughing." Now if someone sucked your titties for some 300 odd years how would you look,
"Perky or Droopy"?

I think the affections were real enough between the children and
mammy, but it wasn't all. It weren't like mother and child.
A slave who settled in Windsor, Canada, wrote her mistress that
she loved the white children she had nursed so faithfully, but she
appreciated "breathing free air" more.
Speaking of mammies and wet nurses, it is interesting to note
that in Portugal in the 17th and 18th centuries the Dr. Spocks of
the day argued among themselves as to who made the best wet
nurses, blondes or brunettes.[5]
Dr. Francisco da Fonseca Henriques thought that blondes would
be best. Another early Dr. Spock was for brunettes. He said:

[3] Liz Carpenter, *Ruffles and Flourishes.* Garden City, New York, Doubleday &
Company, Inc., 1970, p. 28.
[4] From a poem by Gyland Kain "The Blue Guerrilla."
[5] Gilberto Freyre, *The Masters and the Slaves.* New York: Knopf, 1964, p. 381.

". . . In addition to being more full-blooded, they are better able to convert their nourishment into blood and milk, in the manner of the earth, which is the more fertile the blacker it is."[6]

The Portuguese who colonized Brazil must have felt that their children would grow best behind being suckled at the breast of a "Negro" slave because, as Freyre says, the breasts of the Negroes were "the color of the best farming land in the colony."

Dr. J. B. A. Imbert in his medical guide (18th century) commented on the "wet nurse problem."

". . . The breasts should be suitably developed, neither rigid nor flaccid, the tips not too pointed and not too blunt, but adapted to child's lip."[7]

Dr. Imbert figures slaves should be wet nurses cause "as a general rule Brazilian mothers who are still very young

". . . are (not) able to endure the fatigue of a prolonged period of nursing without grave detriment to their own health as well as that of their children."[8]

Mammy not only cooked, but she cleaned her way to freedom. You might say she cleaned the very assholes of America. America has sucked Mammy dry. America's mother is a mammy.

America, honor Mammy Delcie, Mammy Susie, Mammy Chloe, and all the other nameless mammies, who gave their motherhood.

American Negroes who are so proud that "My people were never slaves—they were from Boston, Ohio, or Canada . . ." Did it ever occur to you that maybe the road they traveled was the U.G.R.R., and that Mammy Harriet was the conductor? Name your next child Harriet!

Honor Mammy Sojourner Truth, who traveled all over this land rapping the truth.

Sister Sojourner once met mammy's best friend, Abe Lincoln. When

[6] Ibid., p. 381.
[7] Ibid., p. 381.
[8] Ibid., p. 381.

she met him, she asked him to sign her book in which she kept the names of interesting people that she met. He wrote, "For Aunty Sojourner Truth, October 29, 1864. A. Lincoln." Aunty and Uncle is what W.F.'s call you when they don't wanna say nigger or nigra, and aint about to call you Mr. or Mrs.

Did you know that THE Aunty and Uncle of all, Aunt Jemima and Uncle Ben, were born in Europe? No? No, I don't mean they are European, but the idea of Blacks (Moors) serving goes back to an early European tradition. Since the Emancipation Proclamation and high wages took them out of your kitchen, least you can do is have them on the box cover.

On the subject of Blacks on boxes, Dick Gregory says:

". . . Picture them in your mind. Uncle Ben is clean, he wears a tuxedo, and he is not fat. Do you think it is an accident that advertisers make the black male more attractive than the black female? You have never seen them use a fat, out of shape hillbilly white woman to advertise anything."[9]

In order to maintain the credibility gap I would like to mention a discovery. Brother Dick, W.F.'s must have read your article and got on their case! Aunt Jemima is younger, lighter, and slimmer these days. And her head rag is not a rag anymore. It's a headband, and if you look closely you will see a bit of straight dark brown hair showing. But Quaker Oats blew it, cause on the syrup (next to the pancake) she is shown with the original head rag. Check it out. And Ben done gone. He was replaced by a picture of rice and a pepper mill. So when your grocer gives you a box of rice with Ben on it, you say "Uncle." Cause that means it has been in stock a long time. Aunt Caroline is gone, too. She's been replaced by a rice photo. It is interesting that Aunt Caroline and Uncle Ben, respectfully, were lighter than Aunt Jemima. Uncle Ben looked like a sleeping car porter. That look is the epitome of the loyal house servant. At your service, massa, is what it says. Look at that smile. You know everything is all right and God is in His heaven, long as you can look up and see a nigger smiling and serving. I don't know the

[9] *Ebony*, October, 1971.

name of the brother on the Cream of Wheat box, but he too has that happy-to-serve-you-this-morning, suh, smile.

We have our Uncle Ben and Aunt Jemima and Aunt Caroline, respectively, but France has her Black man on the Banania (a kind of cereal) box, a Black boy eating cassava (manioc), and there is a picture of the French Aunt Caroline on a sugar box. Her head is tied up in one of those many-cornered kerchiefs the women from Martinique do.

While I'm speaking of Uncle and Aunty, lemme run this rap on you. Recently, I purchased a box of washing powder for $5.00. Gold Dust. Are you hip to the Gold Dust twins? Two small, frail looking, bald-headed Black boys who wash a heap of dishes, big skillets, tons of laundry, tile floors, iceboxes, staircases, oilcloths, stoves, sinks, etc. They clean hell out of your house. As a matter of fact, it's written on the box "Let the twins do your work." A friend of mine said that the Gold Dust twins were Aunt Jemima's children by Uncle Ben, and that they were too dark to work serving, so they did the dirty work.

The effect of the Gold Dust twins, Uncle Ben, Aunt Jemima on the Black mind has been negative. Dick Gregory calls it subtle and insidious mental abuse. "A walk through the ghetto supermarket is a study in such mental abuse,"[10] says he. I know what he means. A few years ago I was shopping in the A&P on East 23rd Street. It's quite a ways out of my neighborhood but the food is better, the selection is better, and things are usually marked correctly. That is, a chicken that is advertised at 29¢ a pound is not marked 35¢ in the case. Anyhow I was shopping and I stopped to check my cart. Now it turned out that I stopped right by the Aunt Jemima shelf. A white lady with a baby was passing. The baby looked at me, looked at the pancake boxes on the shelf, looked back at me and said, "Look Ma, the real Aunt Jemima!"

[10] Ibid.

IV

"I just growed"
——Topsy

Mammy was so busy taking care of massa's children, there was no time for her to take care of her own. Aint no wonder Topsy just growed.

"Negro women were too valuable in the field to be allowed much time to care for their children. A month or so after the birth of a child, the mother returned to her task."[1]

Mammy had to nurse and make babies. Big black bellies were a joy to massa. More slaves, more money. It was not important who planted the seed. To quote Joaquin Nabuco, who quotes a manifesto issued by slave-holding planters in Brazil, "The most productive feature of slave property is the generative belly."

"They would buy a fine girl and then a fine man and just put them together like cattle; they would not stop to marry them. If she was a good breeder, they was proud of her. I was stout and they were saving me for a breeding woman but by the time I was big enough I was free . . ."[2]

"I used to tend the nursling thread. The reason they called it that was when the mammies was confined with babies having to suck, they had to spin. I'd take them the thread and bring

[1] Charles S. Sydnor, *Slavery in Mississippi*. Baton Rouge: Louisiana State University Press, 1966, p. 64.
[2] Social Science Institute, *The Unwritten History of Slavery*, p. 1.

it back to the house when it was spinned. If they didn't spin seven or eight cuts a day, they'd git a whupping. It was considerable hard on a woman when she had a fretting baby. But every morning them babies had to be took to the big house, so the white folks could see if they's dressed right. They was money tied up in little nigger young-uns."[3]

[3] B. A. Botkin, *Lay My Burden Down: A Folk History of Slavery.* Chicago: University of Chicago Press, 1945, p. 85.

Mammy the cook was also a mother and often saw her child whipped or treated mean by the white children. She had no way to retaliate except through her work. Lots of times what massa thought was peppercorns were rabbit droppings. Spit was the most common additive. Pee in the bathwater, water too hot or too cold, was very common.

"Stealing" the food was common. Many a mammy was whipped for stealing a biscuit. The same biscuit that she whipped for 500 strokes to make light as a feather. Sometimes Topsy would "steal" the biscuit and suffer the consequences.

"I recollect once when I was trying to clean the house like Old Miss tell me, I finds a biscuit, and I's so hungry I et it, 'cause we never see such a thing as a biscuit only sometimes on Sunday morning. We just have corn bread and syrup and sometimes fat bacon, but when I et that biscuit and she comes in and say, 'Where that biscuit?' I say, 'Miss, I et it 'cause I's so hungry.' Then she grab that broom and start to beating me over the head with it and calling me low-down nigger, and I guess I just clean lost my head 'cause I knowed better than to fight her if I knowed anything 't all, but I start to fight her, and the driver, he comes in and he grabs me and starts beating me with that cat-o'-nine-tails, and he beats me till I fell to the floor nearly dead. He cut my back all to pieces, then they rubs salt in the cuts for more punishment. Lord, Lord, honey! Them was awful days. When Old Master come to the house, he say, 'What you beat that nigger like that for?' And the driver tells him why, and he say, 'She can't work now for a week. She pay for several biscuits in that time.' "[4]

[4] Ibid., pp. 89–90.

Sometimes mammy was abused by the same lil baby she had nursed. In fact, the young white children were encouraged to "keep the niggers straight."

Sister Ellen Cragin, who was a slave in Mississippi, tells us about her mother, who worked at the loom.

"She worked so long and so often that she went to sleep at loom. Master's son saw her and went and told his mother. Mistress said, 'Take a whip and wear her out.' Young master took a stick and beat my mother till she woke up. When she woke up, she took a pole out the loom and beat him nearly to death with it. Young massa begged not to be beat anymore and had the presence of mind to try to make a deal. He said, 'Don't beat me no more and I won't let em whip you.'" Sister Cragin says that her mother replied, "I'm going to kill you. These black titties suckled you and then you come out here to beat me."[5]

Young massa was whupped so bad he wasn't able to walk. Sister Cragin says that her mother then went out and got an old cow named Dolly and "she rode away from the plantation because she knew they would kill her if she stayed. And that was the last I seen of her until after freedom."[6]

Like a friend of mine says, "Slavery is when you suckle babies of the enemy and they grow up into strong and healthy oppressors."

The white children that mammy took care of were full of bad habits. They were nasty, brutal little brats . . . and they chewed tobacco. "The little girls in these parts about seven or eight years old chew tobacco like veterans and babies smoke before they are weaned. The children swear and smoke precociously . . . children get blasé at ten."[7]

The masters delighted in their sons being "chips off the old block." It was not unusual for young masters at age 12 and 13 to "take" a slave concubine. Many, many times the young masters would father

[5] Ibid., p. 174.
[6] Ibid.
[7] Quoted in Bell Irvin Wiley, *The Life of Billy Yank*. Garden City: Doubleday & Company, Inc., 1971, pp. 101–2.

children by their slave half sisters. Slavery produced "a perverted sense of human relationships" in male and female children. Of course, it was mammy and her children who got blamed for the bad habits of the white children.

> . . . It was rarely that he grew up without young Negro lads around him as his playmates. It was from them and from the Negro pantry-girls that he learned obscenity; and it was not long before he lost his virgin purity.[8]
> This happened to many a lad while his mother was still alive; while she was still lively and energetic and kept busy having depraved Negroes or shameless Negro women punished for teaching her children such things. As for those who had no mother, nor stepmother, nor grandmother, it can be imagined how they fared; they were left to the *mucamas,* who were by no means capable always of taking a mother's place.[9]

Many of the Brazilian white women were married off at 12 and 13. Lots of them died shortly after marriage in childbirth.

Lots of times the slave girl would continue to serve the master after his marriage. She would nurse his children by his wife and her. Many a master had nothing but a marriage in name only to a white woman. Some were so hung up on slave women they never married at all.

Sometimes before massa could get it up for his wife, he had a slave woman "excite" him. Some slave women were kept in the house for just this purpose. In one case, the massa had a bad problem and had to have the odor of his favorite slave girl.

> . . . a young man of a well-known slave-holding family in the south. It was necessary for this youth, in order to excite himself for his white bride, to take with him to the bedroom the sweaty nightgown, imbued with the . . . odor of the Negro slave girl with whom he had been having an affair.[10]

Please note at that time, etiquette books "advised young ladies of social standing not to mix books by masculine and feminine writers on the same shelf. Each sex must have a shelf of its own. In good

---

[8] Freyre, *The Masters and the Slaves,* p. 366.
[9] Ibid., p. 367.
[10] Ibid., p. 279.

society one did not speak, either in England or in the United States, of the leg of a table or a chair, but avoided the sensual suggestion of a woman's leg"[11]—yet these same people of upstanding social conscience committed sadistic and perverted sexual crimes on their slaves.

Many a slave (male and female) who had been a playmate of the master in childhood found that in adolescence they now had to play sexual games.

Not a few of the masters were sadists, homosexuals, sodomists and just plain freaks.

> "When Miss Jane's husband died, he willed the niggers to his children, and Mandy Paine owned me then. When I was one month old they said I was so white Mandy Paine thought her brother was my father, so she got me and carried me to the meat block and was going to cut my head off. When the children heard, they run and cried, 'Mama's going to kill Harriet's baby.' Old Mistress, Jane Davis, heard about it, and she come and paid Miss Jane $40 for me and carried me to her home, and I slept right in the bed with her till the war ceasted.
>
> "Her children was grown, and they used to come by and say, 'Ma, why don't you take that nigger out of your bed?' and she'd reach over and pat me and say, 'This the only nigger I got.' "[12]

I find that weird. No weirder perhaps than that play I was in in 1960 on Broadway, *Mandingo*. The hero of this mello drama was a dude who had slave twins for foot warmers. They were named Alpha and Omega. The play was based on a book which the author says was based on historical facts.

[11] Botkin, *Lay My Burden Down*, p. 139.
[12] Ibid., p. 140.

Some of the perversities of slavery will never be told.

"The Old South abounded in wholesale amalgamation—in casual rapes and concubinage, in polygamy and polyandry, in prostitution, and interracial incest. The moral results of slavery, an old planter told author Frederick Bancroft, in its most revealing aspects are unprintable."[13]

Slaves were also given to female children and it seems the female developed the more sadistic and masochistic tendencies. Freyre suggests that it was due to the greater fixity and monotony in the relationship of mistress and slave girl. Many slave narratives slaves bear out the fact that the "mistress" was the "worstest."

Brother Elijah Shaw, a passenger on the underground railroad, reported to William Still and others at the station in Philadelphia that he had not found too much fault with his master "but of his wife he could not speak so favorably"; indeed, he described her as a most tyrannical woman. Said Elijah,

"she would make a practice of rapping the brookstick around the heads of either men, women, or children when she got raised, which was pretty often. She was as mischievous and stingy as she could live; wouldn't give enough to eat or wear."[14]

Brother John Wesley, also a U.G.R.R. passenger, told of several cases of abuses to slaves by the "mistress" on his plantation. One he relates is abuse to a child.

"Another case," said John Wesley, "was a little girl, half-grown, who was washing windows upstairs one day, and unluckily fell asleep in the window, and in this position was found by her mistress; in a rage the mistress hit her a heavy slap, knocked her out of the window, and she fell to the pavement, and died in a few hours from the effects thereof. The mistress professed to know nothing about it, simply said, 'she went to sleep and fell out herself.' As usual nothing was done in the way of punishment."[15]

[13] Lerone Bennett, *Before the Mayflower*. New York: Penguin, 1964, p. 250.
[14] William Still, *The Underground Railroad*. Chicago: Johnson Publishing, 1970, p. 477.
[15] Ibid., p. 477.

To tell you the truth, I can't understand how a society where human beings were held as chattel, where father sold child, where brother raped sister (mulatto and white), where men, women and children were humiliated and mutilated, could produce the delicate, magnolia-smelling, honey-voiced, virtuous, pure, white woman. That's just it. To tell you the truth, she for the most part did not exist. She certainly did not have a sweet 'n' low honey voice. What with all that screaming and shouting at the slaves, she must have ruined her voice box.

". . . For that matter, they might have observed the same thing in the South of the United States, which underwent social and economic influences so similar to those that acted upon Brazil under the regime of slave labor. Even today, owing to the effect of generations of slave-holding ancestors, the young ladies of the Carolinas, of Mississippi and Alabama, are in the habit of shouting just as the daughters and granddaughters of plantation-owners do in northwestern Brazil."[16]

Missy certainly didn't have a lot to do. Mammy took care of the children, Aunty ran the mansion and Sapphire Sallie slept with her husband. Missy was miserable.

One of her biggest and most frequent sources of unhappiness was the yellow pickaninnies born on the plantation. She reacted in many different ways. Sometimes she killed the babies outright. Sometimes she was just mean to them. Sometimes she left her husband. Lots of times missy would not allow the pickaninnies to serve in the house.

". . . there wasn't but one family of half-white children on our place. The old lady would be meaner to them than she was to the black ones. Some of them was marster's chillen and old mistress would not have one of them for a house servant. She would get one right black and wouldn't have none of them in there looking as white as her."[17]

The children with straight hair would get special treatment. Sometimes missy would have it all cut off. Other times she would make them keep it covered, or she would call it out its name.

[16] Freyre, *The Masters and the Slaves*, p. 351.
[17] Social Science Institute, *The Unwritten History of Slavery*, p. 132.

"I had straight hair, and my mistress would say, 'Don't say hair, say wool.' They wouldn't let her mistreat me on account of conditions." (In answer to question of mistress' mistreating him because of kinship, the son says she used to pull out handfuls of his father's hair at times.) . . .[18]

Often the half-white children were the first to be sold. Missy herself would sell them while massa was away (while he was home, too) if she had a particular grudge going with the mother.

Massa himself would sell his slave children quick and soon as any other niggers. It was uncommon for him not to. Massa and missy made a hell of a couple. Six of one and half dozen of the other.

Mr. P. was given to "intemperance," to a very great extent, and gross "profanity." He buys and sells many slaves in the course of the year. "His wife is cross and peevish." She used to take great pleasure in "torturing" one "little slave boy." He was the son of his master (and was owned by him); this was the chief cause of the mistress' spite.[19]

A sister who was an ex-slave talks about the half-white children situation on her plantation.

"Dr. Gale (her master) had about 25 up here in Tennessee, but I reckon he had thousands in Mississippi, and lots of them was his children. They had (his children) to work just like we did and they had to call him marster too; and the overseer would take them down and whip them just like the others. My grandfather was an Irishman and he was a foreman, but he had to whip his children and grandchildren just like the others . . ."[20]

It's hard to say who bothered missy the most—the half-white children, or their mother. Many atrocities were committed by missy against the female slave. Some were beaten for no other reason than to mar their "good looks."

There has always been a "sexual jealousy" on the part of the mistress toward the slave women. Many times the wife would not allow the planter to buy young mulatto female slaves. One wife at a slave

[18] Ibid., p. 37.
[19] Still, *The Underground Railroad*.
[20] Social Science Institute, *The Unwritten History of Slavery*, p. 2.

auction, was overheard to say to her husband, "No, don't buy her, I'll not have that yellow bitch in my house."

The pure African slave woman was also a threat. In some ways— more of a threat, cause it was African and white that made the "mulatto." There have been many cases of the mistress flogging, and breaking the spirit of slaves who were "pure black with the gait of a princess."

> . . . There are tales of *sinhamocas* who had the eyes of pretty *mucamas* gouged out and then had them served to their husbands for dessert, in a jelly-dish, floating in blood that was still fresh.[21]

> . . . the motive, almost always, was jealousy of the husband. Sexual rancor. The rivalry of woman with woman.[22]

Some cut off the breasts of slaves. Some would have the teeth of female slaves, whom they thought the husband had a thing for, pulled or knocked out.

The thing about the teeth is heavy, cause the European women in Europe and the colonies had a serious dental problem.

> ". . . among the white ladies it was rare to find one with good teeth, and on the basis of the colonial chronicles, anecdotes, and traditions it may be asserted that this was one of the principal causes of jealousy and sexual rivalry between the senhoras and the *mucamas*."[23]

Teeth and figures were important for a slave girl. A "For Sale" ad in *Diario de Pernambuco*, the oldest daily paper in Latin America, said . . . "Catarina, of the Benguella tribe, tall, heavy-set, upstanding breasts, broad face, thick lips, *prominent teeth*, very black, *pretty figure*" (October 9, 1838).[24]

Most of the Africans had strong white teeth. Planters always made the slaves open their mouths to show their teeth. It just oc-

[21] Freyre, *The Masters and the Slaves*, p. 351.
[22] Ibid., p. 320.
[23] Ibid., p. 351.
[24] Ibid., p. 381.

curred to me that it is usually white people who flip out over my teeth. "Oh, are those teeth yours!" "Oh, what fantastic teeth you have!" "Oh, your teeth are so white!" Yeah, de is all mine and the better to bite you, massa.

And then came the war and poor missy lost mammy, aunty, pickaninnies and all. Including her reputation. The Yankee soldiers talked about her like a dog. "Southern women often were the special targets of the Yankee disparagers. Some Yanks thought the 'Secesh' women, as they usually referred to them, forward and immodest (one offered in evidence their overfondness for kissing games), while others condemned them as coarse and immoral."[25]

The southern belle was something to write home about. One of them damn Yankee boys wrote home and said that she was a poor looking thing and "I would as soon kiss a dried codfish as one of them." Others talked about her lack of accomplishment in household duties, the crudeness of her speech and her lack of education, and her tobacco habit. One soldier said, "These women here have so disgusted me with their use of tobacco that I am determined to abandon it." One Yankee stationed in Mississippi wrote home:

"[They are] sharp-nosed, tobacco-chewing, snuff-rubbing, flax-headed, hatchet-faced, yellow-eyed, sallow-skinned, cotton-dressed, flat-breasted, bare-headed, long-waisted, hump-shouldered, stoop-necked, big-footed, straddle-toed, sharp-shinned, thin-lipped, pale-faced, lantern-jawed, silly-looking damsels."[26]

[25] Wiley, *The Life of Billy Yank*, p. 100.
[26] Ibid., p. 101.

V

"House niggers aint shit"

Talking bout the plantation, in the summer of '70, Bob Fletcher and I went to Charleston, S.C., to do a story on the low-lands for *Tuesday* magazine. We covered the South Carolina Tricentennial celebration and visited a few plantations. At the Boone Hall plantation, Bob and I brought cotton bolls, mammy dolls, foodstuff, bearing the label "Slave Recipes an original product of old slave mart confections" and a bunch of postcards. We took rolls of pictures. It was funny to see the other tourists' faces, cause they couldn't figure out what we were doing there. They acted like they were very embarrassed. Bob and I were probably "militant looking" to them and yet we walked around smiling all the time. Once I almost cried though, cause as we were approaching the big house, up The Avenue of the Oaks (you know The Avenue—same one Rhett used in *Gone With the Wind*) at the window I saw a short plump woman who looked just like Butterfly McQueen, dusting the table. I screamed, "Bob, did you see that!" She saw us coming and disappeared. When we went inside the big house we didn't see her again. Still I was sad. What a trip to be the housekeeper on a tourist plantation.

We did Boone Hall and moved on to the Middleton Place Gardens. The grounds themselves of both plantations were beautiful, the live oak trees, the flowers, etc. South Carolina by nature is beautiful; but it really was a bit creepy to be walking around the plantation in 1970 acting like it didn't/don't matter. At Middleton Place, we ran into an elderly Black woman who was giving a lecture on the farm implements. Bob took her picture. Middleton Place was one of them sho nuff plantations; had everything going for it right on it.

A world unto itself. Slaves produced everything needed for plantation life (rice and other foods, a masonry, a tannery, etc.). Master Middleton had over 3000 slaves. There was a nigger for all occasions.

Next morning we went to the Slave Mart Museum: "The first museum established to save the crafts taught the negroes during slavery."

Downstairs the Gift Shop. Upstairs the Museum. There was an entrance fee of 50¢, but the woman waived it for Bob and I because we were so "interested in everything."

In the Museum we found framed Confederate money, a saber found on James Island, and old percussion cap gun, found leaning against a tree in the Santee Swamp. There were lotsa photos, prints. Photostats of crime, war news, maps, slave tags, slave bills of sale, a sitz bathtub made by slaves for a Mrs. Martha Bechett Seabrook (one of the first white teachers at the Shaw School for Negroes. There were slave-made quilts, a rug "hand woven by a totally blind negro woman." An embrodied petticoat "1840 made by old Aunt Sarah," a household seamstress, a "primitive" painting tagged 1840, by a runaway slave in gratitude to the gentlemen who helped him escape. There are many more such crafty items but the rest you, dear reader, will have to imagine or go see.

Slaves were sold from the upstairs balcony but we couldn't go out there cause a sign on the door read "Please do not go out on the balcony, it could be dangerous." Bob and I stayed inside. Slaves were held in stalls for inspection and numbered and then led out on the balcony. Buyers stood in the yard commonly known as Mulatto Alley.

The Slave Mart Museum has got the damndest dedication I've seen in years.

> "The Slave Mart Museum is dedicated to the memory of the loyal faithful negroes who during and after the war between the states remained with their former owners, nursed the sick and wounded soldiers returning to the ruins of their homes. Protected the widows and fatherless during the Carpetbagger days. To them may all honor be given."

What can I tell you? It's true. Some slaves did vow to protect the plantation and help missy till massa came home.

A white woman wrote somebody somewhere about the servants on her plantation and said:

"In spite of the infamous proclamation our servants are still loyal, and never rendered more cheerful obedience; indeed their interest in our soldiers and anxiety for the return of peace seems as great as our own. During the Christmas week we had two thousand soldiers passing through . . . This, of course, involved much extra cooking, and it being the servants' holiday, we were much distressed that our charity should infringe on their privileges. We, therefore, determined to remunerate them for their trouble, but when I offered them money they seemed quite hurt and said that they wanted to do their part for our soldiers and not having any money could only give their time."[1]

I pray to the god of justice that cook gave them dysentery, or as some call it, "the flux."

". . . A lot of slaves, afflicted with the flux, being about to be landed for sale, he directed the surgeon to stop the anus of each of them with oakum . . . The Jews, when they examine them, oblige them to stand up, in order to see if there be any discharge; and when they do not perceive this appearance, they consider it as a symptom of recovery. In the present instance, such an appearance being prevented, the bargain was struck, and they were accordingly sold."[2]

In my mind's eye I see the next letter missy wrote.

In spite of all we have done for these dirty niggers they have turned against us. I can't trust any of them. Even that high yaller one that looks like Beauregard. The war goes on, and in spite of what you read in the papers and hear from gossip mongers we are winning.
P.S. Had a letter from Beauregard and he says life on the battlefield is most unattractive. He says the negroes use every excuse to evade the instructions and desert their assignments. Beauregard saw one of the soldiers who passed through here Christmas

[1] Wesley and Romero, *Negro Americans in the Civil War*, p. 147.
[2] Daniel B. Mannix and Malcolm Cowley, *Black Cargoes: A History of the Atlantic Slave Trade, 1518–1865*. New York: Viking Press, p. 129.

last, and he told a most depressing tale. Seems that 1,999 of the the 2,000 soldiers got sick and died. Among them General Eaton's son. Young Eaton had a terrible case of the "sickness" and his two body servants John and Jabo were instructed to take care of him. When they found young Eaton, they found his arse hole plugged up. The body servants are said to have run off to the Union side. And after all General Eaton did for John and Jabo. Ought to kill those niggers if, I mean when, the war ends.

Stay cool and don't worry Niggers will never be free.

Peace,

Anne

Anne was wrong. Niggers would be free.

It is said that some slaves knew freedom was coming and was so certain of it that they would even smile while being whipped.

A diary entry by Elbridge Gerry, Jr., in the summer of 1813;

". . . for the blacks in some places refuse to work, and say they shall soon be free, and then the white people must look out. One Negro woman went so far as to steal her mistress's keys, and refused to return them, saying she would soon pay her for old and new."[3]

Needless to say, massa and missy were getting poor service. One servant went so far as to talk back to missy.

. . . A Memphis newspaper reported, in alluding to widespread evidences of unrest in that city, "that a lady a few days ago went into her kitchen, and gave some directions to the negro cook, who impudently replied with a sneer, 'When Frémont's elected, you'll have to sling them pots yourself.' "[4]

Servants in slavery were called house, field and yard niggers. W.F.'s made up the myth that all house niggers were happy and comfortable. And all field and yard niggers were uncivilized and ferocious.

[3] Herbert Aptheker, *American Negro Slave Revolts*, New York: International Publishers, 1943, p. 92.
[4] Ibid., p. 84.

"In both physical and mental life, there was a great difference between the field hands and the domestic servants and town slaves. Undoubtedly, the latter assimilated more than a smattering of the white man's civilization, both good and bad. Field hands, especially on the larger estates, learned how to lift their hats to a white man, to wield the ox-whip, and to guide a plow; otherwise they were little changed by coming to America. They saw the overseer and the planter but seldom conversed with them. Their associates were fellow field hands. Together they remained in a low stage of civilization for generation after generation."[5]

Right bout here I'd like to say something about house niggers. It's a lie that house niggers aint shit. Quiet as it's kept, not every house nigger was a Tom. There are many, many recorded cases of acts of rebellion among house niggers. If there are many, MANY recorded, you know how many are off the record.

The divide and rule formula was used as a method of slave control. Sometimes personal servants became attracted to their "marsters" and tended to identify their interests with "marster's." Often they would spy and tell "marster" who was where, who stole the cookie from the cookie jar, etc. But by no means were all personal or house servants spies and traitors. They were more likely to tell *slaves* of *marster's* news. Lots of times slaves ran away the night before master could sell them. The news having been overheard by a house servant serving the dinner.

It was illegal to teach slaves to read and write. But where there's a will there's a way and, in spite of the law, many house servants learned to read and write.

Many of the house servants who could would write passes for other slaves. House servants who could, read the newspaper and passed the news on to the others. Masters didn't tell slaves that slavery was an issue in the Civil War. Many found this out from the house servants.

W.F.'s made our light skin brothers and sisters who were house servants feel better than us darker skins bloods. They felt they better by virtue of the fact their light skin was closer to massa who was close to God.

[5] Sydnor, *Slavery in Mississippi*, pp. 254–55.

"They taught us to be against one another and no matter where you would go you would always find one that would be tattling and would have the white folks pecking on you. They would be trying to make it soft for themselves . . .

". . . Later when I had grown and could hire out for myself, I would never hire out where there were two or more servants, for they would keep up a disturbance all the time. If you are doing well they'll tell the white folks something to make them mad. You see they trained them that way in slavery time when they came from Africa and it has just come down from generation to generation . . ."[6]

An interesting note is that slave owners didn't just buy any slaves. In other words, they bought by "brands."

Dudes who had rice plantations bought slaves who came from a rice culture in Africa.

The Guinea Negroes were said to be good for domestic service, waiting on tables, etc.

Slaves from Congo and Angola were good for labor in the field.

"Slaves from Cape Verde and Sierra Leone were bad slaves, but comely of body, especially the women."[7]

I read something that was supposed to make me think the "Black Bourgeoisie" are Mandingos:

"Some evidence might even be assembled to show that the Mandingos, a race of traders in Africa and one that was prized in America as house servants, have furnished more than their quota of the new Negro bourgeoisie."[8]

I don't know about all that but I know slaves was in Slavery. A house, field or yard nigger was a *slave*—and a slave is a slave is a slave, as much as Gertrude Stein's rose was a rose. Slavery aint about the house, the field or the yard. Slavery is about to go going through life "constrained to toil for the happiness of others, to make them comfortable, rich, indolent and tyrannical." Slavery is about gittin Freedom.

[6] Social Science Institute, *The Unwritten History of Slavery.*
[7] Mannix and Cowley, *Black Cargoes*, p. 21.
[8] Ibid.

Just before freedom came, new laws were enacted. Slaves' movements were more restricted than ever. Massa tightened up, so to speak.

Idleness and the congregating of slaves in large numbers on Sundays was another source of infection. These were prohibited except under strict surveillance of white men. The gathering of slaves in Charleston from the plantations were prohibited. Police regulations on the plantations became more rigid. In short there was a tightening up all around.[9]

W.F.'s were scared. They blamed the discontent of the servants on many things. Church people said it was because the slaves were not Baptists.

Some of the Southern whites claimed that the Negroes revolted because they were excited over a church squabble; or because they had been too much indulged, especially in being allowed to learn to read and write. The Southern Baptist Convention thought it was because the Negroes were not Baptists.[10]

Masters mistrusted their slaves however genuine in affection and loyalty they might appear. The bondsmen's privileges were curtailed, and the least signs of insubordination were punished.[11]

What I'm trying to say is most W.F.'s just didn't trust niggers, house, field or yard. Those who could took to speaking French at the table. Those house servants whose job it was to fan the flies at the dining room table were also in trouble. They were under strict surveillance lessen while dey was fanning flies, dey was snatching crumbs.

"Crumbs from master's table breed dangerous appetites."[12]

Poison plots were common. As American as apple pie.

Slaves were forbidden to assemble without the permission and presence of responsible whites. *Slaves were not to practice or administer medicine.* You know what that was about.

[9] Joseph C. Carroll, *Slave Insurrections in the United States, 1800–1865.* Westport: Negro Universities Press, 1938, p. 103.

[10] Ibid., p. 103.

[11] Ibid., p. 109.

[12] Len Chandler, Black poet and folk singer.

As early as 1734 some slaves in Jersey were arrested on an alleged plot. They were found with large quantities of poison.

In 1751 in my homestate of South Carolina they made a law, punishable by death without the benefit of clergy, for slaves found guilty of *attempting* to poison white people. It would be interesting to see what disease, ailment, etc., most frequently planters died of. Wouldn't be surprised if it was a combination of meanness and poison. The *fact* that they made the anti-poisoning of W.F.'s law would mean it was happening quite often.

In 1770 old Georgia got in the act and passed one of her own it's-a-crime-for-a-slave-to-attempt-to-poison-his-master laws. They offered slave informers 20 shillings each year until death. Most niggers who informed were found dead in their cells before they could collect a penny.

In 1755 Maryland convicted five slaves for conspiring to poison four different masters. Again, this is minute. More often massa and/or missus would be meeting their maker before the slave would meet de judge.

In Mississippi in 1860 a plan to poison all the white people in Winston County was foiled by the big mouth of a slave.

". . . In Mecklenburg County, a slave named Dick, belonging to John Gregory, was convicted of conspiring to poison his master to death."[13]

And that old Black magic killed some masters, too. Many believed that the African practiced sexual magic, that he was a love sorcerer for the planters. He or she gave advice, herb teas, aphrodisiacs, etc.

Many a planter was given "love potions" that took him right out of this world. "More than one died outright as a result of the African poison in these concoctions."[14]

[13] Ibid., p. 63.
[14] Freyre, *The Masters and the Slaves*.

"DREAMS AND NIGHTMARES . . .
NIGHTMARES . . . DREAMS! OH!
DREAMING THAT THE NEGROES
OF THE SOUTH HAVE TAKEN OVER—
VOTED ALL THE DIXIECRATS
RIGHT OUT OF POWER
COMES THE COLORED HOUR:
MARTIN LUTHER KING IS GOVERNOR OF GEORGIA,
DR. RUFUS CLEMENT HIS CHIEF ADVISOR,
ZELMA   WATSON   GEORGE   THE   HIGH   GRAND
 WORTHY.
IN WHITE PILLARED MANSIONS
SITTING ON THEIR WIDE VERANDAS,
WEALTHY NEGROES HAVE WHITE SERVANTS,
WHITE SHARECROPPERS WORK THE BLACK PLANTA-
TIONS,
AND COLORED CHILDREN HAVE WHITE MAMMIES:
    MAMMY FAUBUS
    MAMMY EASTLAND
    MAMMY PATTERSON.
DEAR, DEAR DARLING OLD WHITE MAMMIES—
SOMETIMES EVEN BURIED WITH OUR FAMILY!
    DEAR OLD
    MAMMY FAUBUS!
CULTURE, THEY SAY, IS A TWO-WAY STREET:
HAND ME MY MINT JULEP, MAMMY.
    MAKE HASTE![15]

"When the Saints
Go Marching In"
joyously for two
full choruses
with maracas . . . .
Langston Hughes

[15] Langston Hughes, Ask Your Mama. Copyright © 1959, 1961 by Langston Hughes. Reprinted by permission of Alfred A. Knopf, Inc.

VI

"Freedom is better
than slavery
and i know cause
i done seed both sides."
—an ex-slave

August 1865:

Child, I'll be on my way to join you soon as I can make a few mo dresses.

I wants to walk in Freedom looking good.

I am borrowing a few pieces of jewelry from Missy.

You should have stuck around. All the years in Slavery would have been worth it to see what happened yestiddy when Missy read us the Proclamation. You should have seed Old Jake. What with young massa gone to the wah, and old massa blind, cripple and deaf, Old Jake dropped the plow handle and started shouting, sound de trumpet, de day of glory is heah.

We is free, free at last.

And if and when the young massa git back, let him do his own hoeing.

I's free, free at last.

And you member Mulatto Mary? Member how she used to dote on Missy? Fo Missy could finish one mint julep, here come Mulatto Mary wid another.

"Heah's your julep, Missy."

"Is Missy too hot?"

"Is there anythin Missy want me to do?"

"Do you wants me to fan you, Missy?"

"Is Missy's dress ironed well nuff fo Missy?"

"Can I do anythin else fo you, Missy?"

"I'll put the butter on yo grits fo you, Missy."

But heah is the one to take the rag off the bush. Ned told Mulatto Mary that they says she is free as they is. At first it seemed like she was deaf as ol massa. Then Missy shouted for her to bring her a mint julep. Mulatto Mary just stood there. Missy called her again and said she would give her one last chance before she (Missy) whupped her. Mulatto Mary keep on a-staring into space. Missy come down the stairs and over to Mary and started shouting and raised her hand. Well suh, before you could say Jefferson Davis's mother, Mulatto Mary slapped Missy and said,

"Ifin you wants a mint julep, you best git it yoself and don't ever raise your voice at me again. Keep my name out your mouth, and ifin the Lord see fit for you to ever have occasion to ask me something again, don't you fix your mouth to say 'Mulatto Mary.' You best call me Sister Mary, coz we got the same daddy."

Well, you could have knocked me over wid a boll of cotton. I never would have believed it. I always figured Mulatto Mary for one of them sho nuff right on house niggers.

Mammy, don't you cook no more. You are free. Freedom. Free of doom.

Freedom was a bitch. A bitch on wheels. A bitch who didn't take no tea for the fever.

"After that, it wasn't long 'fore the war starts, and the master's two boys, Billy and John, jines the army . . .

". . . After two years him gits a letter from Master Billy and him say him be home soon and that John am kilt. Missy starts crying, and the master jumps up and starts cussing the war and him picks up the hot poker and say, 'Free the nigger, will they? I free them.' And he hit my mammy on the neck, and she starts moaning and crying and draps to the floor. There 'twas, the missy a-moaning, my mammy a-mourning, and the master a-cussing loud as him can. Him takes the gun offen the rack and starts for the field, where the niggers am a-working. My sister and I sees that, and we-uns starts running and screamin 'cause we-uns has brothers and sisters in the field. But the good Lord took a hand in that mess, and the master ain't gone far in the field when him draps all of a sudden. The death sets on the master, and the niggers comes running to him. Him can't talk or move, and they tote him in the house. The doctor comes, and the next day the master dies."[1]

[1] Botkin, *Lay My Burden Down*, p. 237.

Freedom was blind justice.

"The plainest thing I recollect was a big drove of the Yankee soldiers—some riding, some walking—come up to the master's house. He was a sorta old man. He was setting in the gallery. He lived in a big log house. He was reading the paper. He throwed back his head and was dead."[2]

[2] Ibid., p. 235.

Freedom was enough to make you cry.

"We didn't know what the war was 'bout, but Master was gone four years . . .

"When Marse come home, he sent for all the slaves. He was sitting in a yard chair, all tuckered out, and shook hands all round, and said he's glad to see us. Then he said, 'I got something to tell you. You is just as free as I is. You don't 'long to nobody but yourselves. We went to the war and fought, but the Yankees done whuup us, and they say the nigger is free. You can go where you wants to go, or you can stay here, just as you likes.' He couldn't help but cry."[3]

[3] Ibid., p. 232.

Freedom made you bend for a lifetime.

"All I knows 'bout how come us was sot free is that folkses said Mr. Jefferson Davis and Mr. Abraham Lincoln got to fighting 'bout us, and Mr. Lincoln's side got the best of Mr. Davis' side in the quarrel. The day they told us that us was free, there was a white man named Mr. Bruce what axed: 'What you say?' They told him 'gain that all the niggers was free. He bent hisself over and never did straighten his body no more. When he died, he was still all bent over. Mr. Bruce done this to show the world how he hated to give his niggers up after they done been sot free."[4]

4 Ibid., p. 230.

Some thought that Freedom was temporary.

". . . It was 'way after freedom that the freedom man come and read the paper and tell us not to work no more 'less us git pay for it. When he gone, Old Mary Adams, she come out. I 'lect what she say as if I just hear her say it. She say, 'Ten years from today I'll have you all back 'gain.' That ten years been over a mighty long time, and she ain't git us back yet, and she dead and gone."[5]

[5] Ibid., p. 231.

The thought of no servants drove some crazy.

"On Sunday morning Old Master sent the house gal and tell us to all come to the house.

"He said: 'What I want to send for you all is to tell you that you are free. You have the privilege to go anywhere you want, but I don't want none of you to leave me now. I wants you-all to stay right with me. If you stay, you must sign to it.'

"I asked him: 'What you want me to sign for? I is free.' "[6]

[6] Ibid., p. 232.

Some slaves left the plantation forever. Some left and came back because they didn't have no place to go. Some ex-masters and ex-slaves hooked up together and worked the land, and that was the birth of sharecropping.

Some slaves just *didn't* leave on G. P.

". . . He went on to my grandpa's house and says, 'Toby, you are free!' He raised up and says, 'You brought me here from Africa and North Carolina, and I going to stay with you long as ever I get something to eat. You got to look after me!' Master Daniel say, 'Well, I ain't running nobody off my place long as they behave.' Pretty nigh every nigger sot tight till he died of the old sets. Master Daniel says to Grandpa, 'Toby, you ain't my nigger.' Grandpa raise up and say, 'I is, too.' "[7]

[7] Ibid., p. 234.

Slaves found out about freedom in many different ways. Some heard it through the grapevine.

> "We niggers wouldn't know nothing about it at all if it hadn't a-been for a little old black, sassy woman in the quarters that was a-talking all the time about 'freedom.' She give our white folks lots of trouble—she was so sassy to them, but they didn't sell her, and she was set free along with us."[8]

[8] Ibid., p. 237.

Some found out about it sooner than massa told 'em.

"I went down to Augusta to the Freedmen's Bureau to see if 'twas true we was free. I reckon there was over a hundred people there. The man got up and stated to the people: 'You all is just as free as I am. You ain't got no mistress and no master. Work when you want."[9]

[9] Ibid., p. 237.

Slaves became landless Negroes with no clothes, cash, or credit. Many slaves walked the freedom road with nothing but the rags on their back.

Sister Anna Miller, born a slave in Kentucky, and who slaved in Kentucky, Missouri, and Texas, said:

"When freedom comes, Master says to us niggers, 'All that wants to go, git now. You has nothing.' And he turns them away, nothing on 'cept old rags. 'Twa'n't enough to cover their body. No hat, no shoes, no underwear."[10]

10 Ibid., p. 233.

Freedom wasn't easy.

"We knowed freedom was on us, but we didn't know what was to come with it. We thought we was going to get rich like the white folks. We thought we was going to be richer than the white folks, 'cause we was stronger and knowed how to work, and the whites didn't, and they didn't have us to work for them any more. But it didn't turn out that way. We soon found out that freedom could make folks proud, but it didn't make 'em rich."[11]

"The niggers can't hardly git used to the idea. When they wants to leave the place, they still go up to the big house for a pass. They just can't understand 'bout the freedom. Old Marse or Missus say, 'You don't need no pass. All you got to do is just take your foot in your hand and go.' "[12]

[11] Ibid.
[12] Ibid., p. 237.

There was much confusion. Everybody had a different idea of
"Freedom." Most painful of all, some slaves didn't know what "Freedom" was:

". . . They seemed to want to get closer to freedom, so they'd
know what it was—like it was a place or a city."[13]

[13] Ibid., p. 223.

VII

Massas and
lawn Moors

W.F.'s got a massa complex. They got some kinda serve me colored peoples of the world hang up. Probably why the white indentured servant thing didn't last. In the old country, most of 'em were the niggers in their society and they envied royalty, the nobles, the dukes, the earls, etc., being served by Moors. So they took this place and had white servants, some from their own home towns, they didn't feel like they were into nothing. They decided they'd get some more Moors so they could feel like real lords. That's what's behind their penchant for lawn Moors stuck in front of their houses.

When he set out to civilize the world, the European had certain habits that make you question his "civilizing" qualifications!

In the early 19th Century a dude named Robert H. Lowie, in a book he called *Are We Civilized?* tells us:

". . . there were still to be met with in Germany persons who in all their lifetime could not remember having taken a single bath."[1]

We further learn that the Queen Marguerite of Navarre would go for a week without washing her hands. We find out that Louis XIV wasn't too fond of that ritual either, but occasionally would make an effort, and when he did, it was "with a little perfumed alcohol and then he merely sprinkled them." The French even had an etiquette manual (17th Century) that advised the reader not to blow his nose with the hand that was holding a piece of meat. They also had a treatise that gave a recipe for the treatment of lice, which was said to be common all over Europe.

[1] Freyre, *The Masters and the Slaves*, p. 113.

So we learn that this same character who "discovered" America and called the indigenous people "savages" was in reality the funky man out to funk up the world.

The degenerate master psyche is due in part to the fact that Europeans seem to have a problem with hot climates. Look like they get sun stroke and go crazy, be it Kenya, Georgia, Jamaica, India, the tropics does a job on their minds. Remember those movies about Zanzibar? A dude was always sitting on the veranda, served by a native girl whom he'd give a lewd, lingering look to let it be known that she served him in many ways. With tom toms in the background he would always say to the other dude who was usually a newcomer to the tropics, "This is no place for a white man."

In Freyre's *The Masters and Slaves* a point is made that the Dutch had very strong hard feelings "which practically amounted to anti-Semitism" due in part "to the fact that the Israelites acclimated themselves with an astonishing facility, whereas it was extremely difficult for the Flemish to adapt themselves to the life of the tropics."

The European didn't always take his women with him to the colonies, but he always seemed to bring his syphilis.

". . . The disease that laid waste the Old World at the end of the fifteenth century was spread throughout the Orient, having been carried there by the Portuguese. The investigations of Okamura, Dohi, and Susuky, in Japan and in China, and those of Jolly and others in India, show that syphilis appeared in these countries only after they had come into contact with Europeans. In India it made its appearance after the arrival of Vasco da Gama, in 1498, who had sailed from Portugal the year before."[2]

It is customary to say that civilization and syphilis go hand in hand, but Brazil would appear to have been syphilized before it was civilized.[3]

More about the Moors. Europeans had/have very definite images, ideas, myths, and roles for Moors. This section on Europe is a record of domestic service that culminates with the American experience of Black servitude.

[2] Ibid., p. 73.
[3] Ibid., p. 71.

The Europeans were heavy in the slave trade *early*.

By mid-17th Century, "Almost every European nation was by then engaged in it—except the Italians, the Austrians, the Poles, and the Russians, none of whom had colonies—and each nation excused itself by depicting the Africans as hopeless savages, while blaming every other nation for treating them badly."[4]

Queen Elizabeth herself was a shareholder in slaving:

> When Queen Elizabeth heard of Hawkins' slaving venture, she said "It was detestable and would call down vengeance from heaven upon the undertakers." Hawkins went to see the queen and showed Her Majesty his profit sheet. Not only did she forgive him but she became a shareholder in his second slaving voyage.[5]

Seems that slaving ran in the Royal Family.

> . . . In 1663 an English company was chartered under the Duke of York, brother of Charles II, to supply a minimum of three thousand slaves yearly to the new colonies. It had the romantic title of "The Company of Royal Adventurers of England Trading to Africa," and, as a tribute to the duke, its slaves were branded with the letters DY. To advertise the company, in which he had invested money, King Charles had a new coin issued; it was made of gold from West Africa and was called a guinea.[6]

During slavery in Liverpool, slaving was so good, "A new system of docks had to be constructed to hold the ships, and this was the beginning of the docking system that made Liverpool the greatest port in the world."[7]

Liverpool made no secret of the source of its sudden wealth. "The town hall was covered with stone reproductions of elephants' teeth and "blackamoors." Shop windows were full of handcuffs, leg irons, collars, and slave chains for outgoing vessels. Goldsmiths advertised "Silver Locks and Collars for Blacks and Dogs," . . .

[4] Mannix and Cowley, *Black Cargoes.*
[5] Ibid., p. 22.
[6] Ibid., p. 28.
[7] Ibid., p. 73.

. . . The famous actor George Frederick Cooke appeared drunk on the stage of the Theater Royal in Liverpool and was booed by the audience. Reeling to the footlights, he shouted, "I have not come here to be insulted by a set of wretches, every brick in whose infernal town is cemented with an African's blood."[8]

European women walked young Black warriors like they now walk poodles: ". . . ladies of fashion appeared in public each with a monkey dressed in an embroidered jacket and a little black slave boy wearing a turban and baggy silk pantaloons."[9]

Moor men and maid servants were the thing.

Many an Englishman took a Moorish maid to wife and plenty mistresses took to the bed with the butler and valet. Some married. One English matron in 1885, took herself and her children (by an Englishman) and eloped with the butler of color.[10] One Earl found his mistress on the knee of his Moorish footman and promptly packed both off in a carriage to seek their fortune.

All over jolly old England, upper, middle and lower class natives were marrying, hanging out with, sleeping with their servants, long as they were Moor.

The women servants were called maids of honor. One queen went so far as to honor her maid with a day.

Oh, speaking of maid's honor day don't you know that:

May 5, 1971, is Maid's Honor day, as proclaimed by Mayor Sam Massell. The idea for such a day was conceived and is sponsored by the National Domestic Workers' Union of America, of which Mrs. Dorothy Bolden is president.

This day, May 5, 1971, is set aside to honor some 30,000 maids who have rendered many years of faithful service to their employers and will be climaxed with a banquet at 8:00 P.M. at the American Hotel. At this time cash, trophies, citations and many other awards will be presented to Atlanta's top domestic workers nominated for the awards by their employers.[11]

[8] Ibid., p. 74.
[9] Rogers, *Sex and Race.*
[10] Ibid.
[11] Atlanta *Voice*, April 17, 1971.

I wanted to go, but couldn't. I didn't have a babysitter.

Anyhow, back to the Queen who honored a maid.

This particular queen (Margaret of Scotland) had her Moorish maid baptized Elen More (a lot of people with the names Moore, Moorer, Mooris etc., probably got their names from their Moorish ancestors—for instance, Morrison means son of a Moor.)

This thing that masters got about renaming their servants is weird.

In William the Conquerer's time, it was a popular thing for Earls and Dukes to call their valets John Morocco. John for Christian, Morocco for Moor.

In my daughters' school it's popular for the teachers to call Puerto Rican children named Juan, John. A photographer friend of mine told me that his grandmother used to do housework for W.F.'s in Detroit, who kept calling her Delcie, and her name was Margaret. When he asked his grandmother why they called her out of her name, she said, "They call all their maids Delcie."

Another friend of mine who is a well known folk singer, told me that his grandmother worked for some W.F.'s who was also out of her name. Their reason was that the grandmother's name was the same as that of a family friend who had died, and they didn't feel like calling her that.

Calling people out their names is a bad habit the people of European descent seem to have. The one that takes the rag off the bush is how they went all the way to Africa and called nature out of its name . . . Victoria Falls, Leopoldville, Johannesburg, Lake Victoria, Lake Rudolf, Lake Albert, etc. The W.F.'s that came here did the same thing with the indigenous people living here . . . called them Indians; and years later missionaries, government officials, census takers, etc., "tidied up their records and account books by arbitrarily shortening or changing the names of their charges." "He Who Causes Fear" and "Brave Chief" suddenly became Indian Joe and Bob.[12]

Of course, in early Europe not every Moor was a servant, and not every servant was a Moor. Although more Moors were servants, than servants Moors.

Some Moors were gondoliers, tradesmen, physicians and herb sellers. In Europe it was known that the Moor was remarkable in his use

[12] Gilbert Osofsky, ed. *Puttin On Ole Massa: The Slave Narratives of Henry Bibb, William W. Brown, and Solomon Northrup.* New York: Harper & Row, 1969, p. 41.

of the herb. Many times it was the Moor who brewed the tea or potion that cured, when European physicians had pronounced the patient incurable.

Moors were represented everywhere in Europe, on plates, mugs, etc., and on coats of arms. Many a Moor was a favorite. A favorite was a pet of royalty, nobility and well-to-do Europeans.

Most of the courts and rich households had favorites, and it seems the blacker the berry the sweeter the juice. Queen Isabella of Aragon wrote her "nigger" agent in Venice asking him to send her another "nigger," but blacker than the previous one.[13] Madame Du Barry had a black favorite, whom she made the governor of her chateau. His name was Zamor. Indeed, it's reported that she favored Zamor over King Louis XV.

It was quite fashionable to have portraits painted with favorites.

Lampi painted Catherine the Great, high on her horse with her favorite beside the horse.

Titian painted Lucretia Borgia and her "Nigger" favorite.

English painter Hogarth shows an English lady with her lily white hand under her favorite's chin, checking him out—as if to say, "See how cute I dressed you today."

Madame Du Barry was not to be out-done, so she had herself painted with Zamor. Instead of Zamor doing the serving, he was served and fed by the grande dame of the court.

Goya painted the Duchess of Alba and her little favorite, Maria De La Luz. Another Spaniard, Valasquez, painted his servant Juan. Juan can be seen at the New York Metropolitan Museum of Art.

There were servants of color in ancient Rome too. They served as charioteers, bath attendants, cooks, flute players, gladiators, Priests of Isis, wrestlers, waiters, conductors of elephants, and other things like that.

Although there were white servants, colored people brought the highest prices on the slave mart.

To have a number of Ethiopian slaves in one's service was a sign of great luxury in the Imperial epoch; so much so; that they were brought in "droves" to Rome after the Egyptian conquest.[14]

[13] Rogers, *Sex and Race.*
[14] Ibid.

Romans were so taken with servants of color, "Moors," Ethiopians, whatever you want to call them, that they put them everywhere. Figurines of Moors were everywhere, on cameo bracelets, ointment jars and other accessories of grande dames.[15]

On the subject of Romans and Ethiopians, I have an Ethiopian friend and he told me that during the occupation of Ethiopia by the Italians, in the Addis Ababa area, soldiers had a family of servants: that is, families would have their own soldier—not for security, but for serving.

People of color were preferred as intimate servants. Women of color were preferred as wet nurses to the big boys as well as the babies.

The Roman women resented that fact. There were many abuses to the Moorish women by the Roman ladies.

In Pompeii, a brothel called the House of the Rising Sun had graffiti which read . . . "Candide me docuit nigras odisse puellas."[16] Underneath that mouthful was written, "odero Septero Ped invitus amabo," loosely translated means . . . a white girl taught me to hate black girls. You may hate them, but you will return to them.

With so much black around, yellow soon followed. Unlike slavery, when the Black woman had the master's child, the white woman had the servant's baby.[17]

Juvenal in 2nd Century A.D. in attacking Roman wives for general misconduct, one of which is illicit sex relations with the Negroes, he says, "These matrons are likely to bear black children."

Husbands were advised to give their wives abortive potions.

One writer advised the husbands not to grieve at this, but "with thine own hand give the wife the potion, whatever it may be, for did she choose to bear her leaping children in her womb thou wouldst perchance, become the sire of an Ethiop, a black, a Moor would soon be your soul heir."

Many Roman children born were blackamoor than white.

Most of the Roman ladies who gave birth to children of color claimed it was "maternal impression." There was a general misconception in Rome at that time, that a picture or statue, etc., of a black

[15] Ibid.
[16] Ibid.
[17] Ibid.

in the same room at the moment of conception would produce a black child.

It is interesting to note that there is an old Anglo-Saxon myth that seeing a blackamoor the first thing in the morning is an omen of good luck.

When I was a child, I remember my grandmother saying that "seeing a man first thing on a Sunday morning brings good luck." She didn't say nothing about black. I guess cause we were.

I also heared of a midwestern town where white prostitutes on Saturday nights would pay an old Negro to walk through each room to bring good luck.

Misconceptions like good luck, and even chocolate, created Moor babies in Rome, early Europe, and midwest America.

The Queen of France had a baby girl. Many said it looked like one of the black dwarfs in court. The King himself noticed the striking resemblance and mentioned it to the doctor. The doctor told him it was because the Queen drank too much chocolate, and looked too hard at the dwarf. The Queen, the dwarf and the baby had no comment. The baby was sent to the convent for life, the dwarf disappeared, and the Queen never drank another drop of chocolate.

Ethiopians, blackamoor, Moorish, Morrison, Blackmore, Blackburn, all played an important and common role in the servant and sexual life of the peoples of ancient Rome and early Europe.

It was considered so common in Europe to have a Moor favorite, that the 2nd Duke of Dorset, whose family had had Moor pages for generations, decided to change up, and get him a Chinese page, just to be original. Asked why he did such a thing, he said . . . "Everybody had a black one."[18]

And so we can see with that kind of historical, sociological and political image of the Moor in service, the newly arrived European did not feel lord and master until he had got him some Moors to serve him. It's safe to say W.F.'s have a cultural hangover and Uncle Ben is a Super Moor.

[18] Ibid.

VIII

"Nobody knows
the master better
than the servant."
—Malcolm X

Servants is what you get when you fly to Jamaica on "The Wings of Man" (Eastern Airlines) and you can't afford a hotel, so you rent a villa "with a cook who also baby-sits, a maid and a gardener who also takes care of your pool."[1]

A servant is the Black woman who is serving tea to Dame Edith Sitwell, propped up in her canopied bed, being photographed by Sir Cecil Beaton.[2]

A servant is someone who will work on their day off so you can go play bridge. Someone who always knew someone else who would work for you, if they couldn't make it.

A friend of mine told me that she called her mother's employer to tell her that her mother had died over the weekend and would not be able to come in. The employer said "Oh, dear, that is too bad. Could you recommend someone else? The house is a wreck after the weekend."

A servant is sunshine on a cloudy day. A mother's helper. My girl. One sister I talked to said that she quit cause her employer, on the phone, she'd say, "If I'm not here, leave the message with my girl."

[1] Ad in the New York Daily News by Eastern Airlines, Nov. 19, 1971.
[2] Vogue magazine, The World of Vogue, New York: Viking Press, 1963, p. 87.

A "girl" from the South is considered better than a northern "girl"!
A West Indian "girl" is better than both. A Puerto Rican "girl" is
gauche. A Haitian "girl" is exotic. A South American "girl" is fantastic. A Canadian "girl" is marvelous. A French "girl" is a tutor. An
English "girl" is a governess.

Servants is the reason the City of West Palm Beach, Florida, was
established by Henry Morrison Flagler. "No blacks aside from servants have ever lived there (Palm Beach). Until fairly recently any
black found in town after sundown without a good excuse was liable
to get an exemplary beating and at least a night in jail from the
police."[3]

A servant is the sullen chauffeur who pushes the cart for the bargain conscious housewife in Palm Beach, Florida. "It has become
almost fashionable to acknowledge the high cost of living by shopping in supermarkets in West Palm Beach instead of letting the butler
do the shopping from the expensive specialty grocers here. Once a
week scores of Palm Beach chatelaines wander through the aisles of
the publix or Winn-Dixie, looking for the specials while their chauffeurs sullenly push the carts."[4]

Servants servant other servants sometimes. At Mar-A-Lago, a mansion run, owned and managed by Mrs. Marjorie Merriweather Post,
who when asked about her 60 servants (40 work inside and 20 work
outside) said, "You don't expect me to make my own bed, do you?"[5]

> She even thinks that up in heaven
> Her class lies late and snores
> While poor black cherubs rise at seven
> To do celestial chores.[6]

Servants were slaves who cried when massa hit the cold, cold
ground.

[3] New York *Times Magazine*, March 21, 1971.
[4] Ibid.
[5] Ibid.
[6] "For a Lady I Know" in *On These I Stand* by Countee Cullen. New York:
Harper & Row, 1969. Copyright, 1925 by Harper & Row, Publishers, Inc. Re-
newed, 1953 by Ida M. Cullen. By permission of the publishers.

"I remember once when one of the white folks died, ole Uncle Albert keeled over on the floor and was just a crying, but when he saw nobody was looking, he was just a dying laughing."[7]

"Mistress would say, 'Go pick up some chips for old Aunt Fan to put on the lid' and I would run and break out to get the chips first, 'cause I was crazy about white bread and when we all got back with the chips, Mistress would give us some white bread, but she would make me wait till they all got there. I liked it 'cause Mammy 'nem didn't get white bread but once a week—that was Sunday, and the rest of the time they had just corn bread or shorts. I was so foolish! When she died (Mistress) it liked to killed me; I just cried and cried and Mammy say, 'What's the matter with you, gal?' I said, 'Ole Miss is dead, and I won't get no more white bread.' She said, 'Shet you mouth, gal.' I thought when she died she carried all the white bread with her. Folks was saying, 'Look at that po' little nigger crying 'bout her Mistress 'but I wasn't crying 'bout Mistress I was crying 'cause the white bread was gone."[8]

A servant is a flip.

They are on duty in the dining rooms at the Naval Academy and the White House. They man the gallies on U. S. Navy and Coast Guard vessels. They wait on captains and admirals, hand and foot. At first glance, those 15,000 odd Filipinos currently serving as stewards in the U. S. Navy and Coast Guard seem an anachronistic throwback to the white-gloved days of U.S. colonialism.

At sea, the stewards serve officers as personal, all-purpose valets—combination shoeshine boys, dishwashers and cabin boys. Ashore their duties range from ordinary house work in BOQ's to keeping the milk pitchers and serving dishes filled at the Naval Academy mess hall.

The basic pay of a Filipino recruit, runs approximately $1,500 a year—the same pay as a U.S. recruit gets.

Rare is the Filipino steward who has not smarted at becoming a flip (for Filipino) or a moke (from the tagalog word amok).

[7] Social Science Institute, *Unwritten History of Slavery*, p. 68.
[8] Ibid., p. 55.

In any event, neither the Navy nor the Coast Guard has be-
gun recruiting Filipinos for other jobs—a fact that has raised
some eyebrows among liberals in the U.S. But there seems
to be little griping among Filipinos. "I would resent exploitation of Filipino boys in the U. S. Navy," says Manila's Director
of Labor Standards, Ruben Santos. "But there have been no
complaints in this area."[9]

A servant by any other name is a housekeeper, a maid and sometimes a nanny. A nanny is sometimes a governess or a companion.
Most nannies, companions and governesses are of European descent.

Seeings how I aint white or rich, and not being able to be one
or hire one, white nannies are something I can't speak of from first-
hand experience.

Brother *Lift Every Voice And Sing* James Weldon Johnson had
a white nanny.

> "When I was born, my mother was very ill, too ill to nurse
> me. Then she found a friend and neighbor in an unexpected
> quarter. Mrs. McCleary, her white neighbor who lived a block
> away, had a short while before given birth to a girl baby. When
> this baby was christened she was named Angel. The mother of
> Angel, hearing of my mother's plight, took me and nursed me
> at her breast until my mother had recovered sufficiently to give
> me her own milk. So it appears that in the land of black mam-
> mies I had a white one. Between her and me there existed an
> affectionate relation through all my childhood; and even in after
> years when I had grown up and moved away I never, up to the
> time of her death, went back to my old home without paying
> her a visit and taking her some small gift.
>
> I do not intend to boast about a white mammy, for I have
> perceived bad taste in those Southern white people who are con-
> tinually boasting about their black mammies."[10]

The closest and onliest thing to a white nanny in my house was
Maria Ball Hoffman, a white Russian neighbor who lived on the

[9] *Newsweek*, November 9, 1970.
[10] James Weldon Johnson, "Along This Way," in Abraham Chapman, ed.
Black Voices: An Anthology of Afro-American Literature, New York: New American Library, 1968, pp. 271–72.

top floor and believed in homeopathic medicine. She was a house-phone-dog-and-children sitter. She would sit with any one of the fore mentioned for the same price. Unlike Jackie Kennedy and *her* Miss Shaw, I couldn't leave everything for my Maria. I had to clean the house, cook the food, arrange paper & pencil by the phone for messages, put the can opener next to the dog food, etc., before I left the house, and wash the dishes when I got back. Maria didn't wash dishes because she is a peasant by her own admission. She says that my kitchen was too refined for her to work in, so I had to do the dishes. To tell the truth, she would just as soon wash iron frying pans and crystal glasses together. Maria worked out fine as long as she stayed in her place. Things would get sticky when I'd leave home thinking she was sitting for me, and meet my next-door neighbor, who would say, "Maria is sitting for me, who's sitting for you?" We found out that Maria was "monitoring" both apartments. Sometimes she would bring in other children from the building and things would get out of hand. Otherwise Maria was a good baby-sitter. She was very resourceful. She knew how to "make do" and was excellent in case of any kind of emergency. You could say, "Maria, I met an old school friend and I'm stopping to have coffee with them so I won't be at the phone number where I thought I'd be and it's an unlisted number so if they call would you tell them to call Joyce first and I'll call her later to explain what to explain to them." She would say, "Sure."

A servant is usually a person of color.

Quiet as it's kept, there is a certain type of "upper class" white folks who don't use "colored help" at all. In fact, household labor is a segregated occupation. A Lancashire-born (English) butler, asked if he had encountered many black men and women in his 20 years of service, said reflectively, "I can't think of one I worked with. On one job we had an Italian cook, an Irish kitchen man, a French lady's maid, an English butler, and an English parlormaid."

The upper echelon's household staff is 99–99/100% white.

An ex-friend of mine, who comes from all that, told me that his family wouldn't hire nothing but white. His mother said, "I don't want Negroes in my house." My ex-friend's father was an opera freak. But he stopped going to the opera after Leontyne took it.

IN THE POT BEHIND THE
PAPER DOORS WHAT'S COOKING?
WHAT'S SMELLING, LEONTYNE?
LIEDER, LOVELY LIEDER
AND A LEAF OF COLLARD GREEN,
LOVELY LIEDER LEONTYNE."[11]
—Langston Hughes

White House Nanny (one of those "what the butler saw" books) was weird and informative. I learned about rich W.F.'s and about the people who work for them.

For instance, Miss Shaw is unmarried, spent 40 years caring for other people's children. She is now retired, lives in England. One of her treasures is a "gold-embossed, leather bound scrap book" on her bookcase in her home in Kent County, England, with an inscription from Mrs. J. Kennedy which says:

> You brought such happiness to all our lives and especially to President Kennedy, because you made his children what they are.[12]

I have learned that it's not just a matter of money. The rich are different. When President Kennedy died, Miss Shaw was the one to tell Caroline. So different from when my daddy died. My mama told me, held me close and Uncle Zander was there and Aunt Virter and Junior and Mary and my grandmother and we cried together.

Ironically, those rich W.F.'s who live on Park and Fifth Avenue in the 80's and 90's—the establishment, so to speak—the ones who live the closest to Harlem, never go there. For them Harlem is "a light-year away, uptown."

For them "there is Terror in Harlem."

For us, "Harlem is the asphalt plantation of America."[13]

[11] From "Cultural Exchange," in *Ask Your Mama,* by Langston Hughes, p. 6. Copyright © 1959, 1961 by Langston Hughes. Reprinted by permission of Alfred A. Knopf, Inc.

[12] Shaw, *White House Nanny,* p. 7.

[13] From a poem by Calvin Hernton, "Jitterbugging in the Streets," in LeRoi Jones and Roy Neal, eds., *Black Fire.* New York: Morrow, 1968, p. 207.

In New York City, Gramercy and Central are THE parks where the nannies can be found. Funny thing, Gramercy Park, which is a "private" park and is very exclusive more so than any part of Central Park as far as white nannies go, was once owned by a slave of Mrs. Peter Stuyvesant's. Mrs. Stuyvesant sold it to her when it was a swamp. That's another habit W.F.'s have. Always selling something to their servants. Wonder what Gramercy Park would be like if Mrs. Stuyvesant's slave was the landlord today?

I've seen "nannies" in Central Park going through whose carriage is the hippest. One Frenchwoman was strutting like it was her baby in the English carriage. Along comes a English nanny with a Austrian carriage to out-prance her. They were both chagrined when a white American "housekeeper" pushing an American-made copy of a European carriage pranced on.

Some rich W.F.'s have Oriental "houseboys." They even got TV shows about it. In one show, an Oriental houseboy has to take care of the adolescent girl and help the daddy out of all his entanglements that bachelor fathers are prone to get into.

A friend of mine, born and raised in Newport, Rhode Island, told me that once his mother hired a black butler. Well, the truth hit the fan. The Irish upper and downstairs maids, the Scottish couple, the English chauffeur, all got together and told her that they wanted the butler to eat separately and wanted his sheets washed separately. This did not make for good inter-domestic relations, and so she eventually fired the black butler.

Interesting footnote: The husband of the house used to have all, I mean every one of Paul Robeson's records, but when Pearl Bailey married Louis Bellson, he broke them.[14]

[14] New York *Post*, July 14, 1969.

A sister told me she knew of a family in Brooklyn who once had a white maid. This family was very fair-skinned. It wasn't that they were passing, but if they didn't tell you that they were colored, you might think they were white. One day the lady of the house announced to the maid to get the guest room ready, as her brother was coming. The white maid hurried and scurried around and finally the guest arrived. As the maid saw her employer hugging and kissing a brown-skin man, she asked, "What are you people?" We are colored was the reply. "Well, I quit—cause I'd rather work for po white folks than work for niggers."

"Color alone is here [in the South] the badge of distinction, the true mark of aristocracy, and all who are white are equal in spite of the variety of occupation."[15]

White Americans are infamous for giving bad service. They have a rep for being insolent and rude in service jobs.

Lots of travelers, voyaging to Europe, avoid American ships. They say the service stinks.

If you ask the steward to bring you something in your cabin or clean your porthole, he is apt to tell you: "Listen, I'm as good as you. Just because I have this job, don't think I'm here to wait on you. I'm a college graduate and only doing this to get my Masters' Degree. I'm not going to be a steward all my life. I've been more places in Europe than you will ever visit. I'm not your servant. Clean your own porthole." I've found that white service people really go thru changes servicing Black people.

The first thing they do is try to equalize the thing. They gets familiar. See, that ways it's not "about serving" Blacks! It's about being casual. Getting down to the real nitty gritty. Informal. I re-

[15] Kenneth M. Stampp and Leon F. Litwack, eds. *Reconstruction: An Anthology of Revisionist Writings*. Baton Rouge: Louisiana State University Press, 1969, p. 207.

member when the Mayor of Fun City had a reception for the Nicks at Gracie Mansion. It was informal. Hot dogs on the lawn. Cold as it was, a spring lawn party. And that year, spring was *very* late. Everybody was complainin. Getting their gators messed up in the wet grass. And why were the doors to the mansion locked? They even had a white, rag time-rock band. From the git, I sensed that the party was going to be a dud. Anytime you go to all that trouble to make up fancy invitations—and when the guests arrive, you just say "You here for the party?"—you know somethin aint Kosher. I guess we all looked alike to him, and it wasn't worth going through the ritual of checking invites, being exclusive, etc. It was informal!

Taxis drivers do that all the time. Plus they get funny. One time I was going to visit a friend in the hospital and I was in a hurry. So I got a taxi and told him where I wanted to go, and asked him to take the fastest way. He llows, "Don't worry, he'll wait."

Since the new taxi rates in New York City, more taxis stop for Black folks. They so hungry now that the Yellow Cabs outside of the Bickford's Restaurant on Jerome and Burnside Avenues in the Bronx, are carrying stickers saying: "Let's Be Friends!" They are lucky to get any riders. A Black comedian on TV said: "Tonight I was standing on the corner and a taxi stopped and asked me if I wanted to go to Harlem."

On the other hand, white riders expect the Black taxi drivers to act like chauffeurs.

Restaurants, fancy ones in particular, are really guilty of that getting familiar routine. When I'm eating in a restaurant full of people, how come I'm honey, and they are sir or madam? I discourage that stuff, before they go too far. Last time a waiter went into that routine with me: "Is everything okay, honey. bet your old man likes you, honey. do you want more coffee, honey . . . honey dis, honey dat." Just call me Madam, if you please.

Since I've been in the book business, I go out to lunch a lot. Especially, in the "best" restaurants. I have noticed "racism in the kitchen." You'd be sitting there, and before you could finish your expresso, out comes a dark skinned bus boy. Usually, a Puerto Rican. The kitchen doors swing open, one can't help but notice that the suds busters are dark too.

One time I was in New York's finest Italian restaurant, and as I looked around at the pasta, I said: "Yeah, think I'll open me a joint somewhere round here." "Oh, no," my white companions said, "it wouldn't work, there aren't enough black people working around here to support a soul food restaurant." I said, "Are all the people in here Italian? Do all the people who eat in Le Pavillon speak French?" It's about prime real estate. "What you mean is that I couldn't *get* a restaurant round here." And that is how it bes.

It's all about some money, honey, and if that aint so, how come it aint *Carver* Chunky Peanut Butter?

White women who have the service jobs are the worst.

I noticed when W.F.'s gave up the train and took to flying, your "service" was provided by Cheryl, Sharon and Barbara, all smiling white girls. The W.F.'s acted like they wasn't never gonna hire Black airline stewardesses. Why? Were W.F.'s tired of Black folks serving them? Suddenly they didn't want us close to them, standing over them in the air? Well, for one, airline stewardess is a good paying job. But it's the occupational hazard of stewardesses—marriage. In the beginning stewardesses were really out to "serve" you, but now— what with European designers doing their sky outfits and buffet eating, they have developed attitudes and you get more negative vibrations than good service.

There are agencies on the East Side of New York that only handle European help. I decided to go and try my luck with the fanciest one. I went in with my wig, a banlon pants suit, and said, "I, am looking for a housework job." There were not even raised eyebrows as the woman, a middle aged blonde with a bun on the back of her head, said, "We have nothing for you—no calls have come in yet today." I told her I would wait and I did. I waited for several hours and then I asked if I could use the bathroom. She said that across the street was a Horn and Hardart Automat, and I could use the "restroom" there. I told her I would prefer to use the one in the agency, cause a call might come while I was gone. I said, "I know you got a bathroom here cause you got to go sometime, don't you!" She handed me a key and said "go down the hall to your right, be sure and lock it back when you finish and please be sure to flush." I said, "Oh don't worry, I'm only going to do number one." Only then, did she show a little blush in her face. When I came back, I asked if any calls had come for me and she said no. The whole three hours I spent there the phone was lighting up every five minutes. Finally, I said, "I'm gonna cross the street to get something to eat at your Automat, I'll be back." I took a cab and went home. I took a cab, because I was afraid that on a bus or subway, I'd run into someone I knew who'd say—what the hell are you doing wearing that wig?

I knew a rich white lady on Park Avenue, and decided to ask her to call the agency and ask for a governess. She made the appointment for Wednesday of the next week, and the thing was, when the governess came for the interview, I'd be she, the rich white lady. Well, Wednesday of the next week I arrived at 10:00. Hazel, the Black maid, and I removed all photos and paintings of the white family off walls, pianos, dishes, tables, etc. I got dressed in an ultra-super, sophisticated pants suit that I had made the night before, just for the occasion. 11:00 A.M. came, and I was a rich white lady for a day. Everything went smoothly, cause when the girl (and she was just that) arrived and told the doorman "Mrs. Bowser," he smiled and said, "of course, Apartment 3 N.E."!

The bell rang, Hazel answered and the girl threw a look at Hazel. Hazel said to me later, "When she came in, she didn't deal with me because I was Black and only a maid, and she was white and would be the governess. I thought to myself, just you wait honey—just you wait." Hazel took her coat, showed her into the living room, and said . . . "Mrs. B. will be with you in a minute."

How can I describe that minute? The minute the poor girl saw me, an adam's apple popped out on her neck, her face turned, not even a color—it just turned. She had gotten up, but froze in mid-air. I felt sorry for her. She looked ill. I put out my hand and said, "How do you do, so good of you to come." She was still in mid-air, and I told her, "sit down, please, and tell me all about yourself." The girl said, "Well, mum, I'm 20." I said, "you're Irish too, aren't you?" She said, "Yes mum." "How long have you been here?" I asked. "About a month." At that moment, by previous arrangement, Hazel came in with a silver tray of coffee. I offered Elizabeth (the girl) some, and she said . . . "Oh, no, no." I said, "Oh, you don't drink coffee? I just love Irish coffee myself." As Hazel was leaving, I yelled, "Oh Hazel, have we any crackers?" "No," she answered, "Just Oreos." I turned my attention back to the girl, and asked her, "Why did you come to America?" At this point, I gotta tell you that her eyes never left me. She was sitting in a chair facing me, and she had now turned green with fright (although it might have been envy). "Left Ireland to better myself," she said. "I've got two sisters here. One on 86th Street, and the other on 91st." "Oh, they live close by," I said. "It's not their home, Mum, they're in service." "Well, continue. Tell me about the rest of your family." "My father is a carpenter, and my mother is a lady who had 16 children. I'm the next to the youngest." "Do you have any children?" "Oh no Mum, I'm not even married." "These days one never can tell. It doesn't matter to some, you know."

"By the way," I said, "we are Protestants. Does that make a difference?" "Oh no, *that* doesn't make any difference," she said. Then we talked about the job, and what I expected of her.

"Did the agency tell you that there were seven children?" "Seven?" "Oh yes," I said. "Most of them are away. Primarily, I want you to deal with Jamie. Take him back and forth to school, make his dinner, read to him. You can read, can't you?" She blushed, and said, "Well, yes Mum, I can read children's books well enough, if they are in simple English." "Well, never mind. Jamie watches 'Sesame Street' every day, and will probably be able to help you out. He's terribly precocious. You'd never know he was five. By the way, Jamie is Chinese." "Chinese !" she said. "Yes, and speaks it too. ALL of the children are something. Eric is Cambodian, Sarah is Sudanese, Maria Therese is a Chicano, Jose is a Seminole, Edward is a Blackfoot, and Ezekiel is a Puerto Rican."

By this time, the girl's adam's apple was racing up and down, and she looked like she was going to faint. I asked her if I could get her something—a drink of water, or whiskey. She shook her head. Then I said, "Oh, I must ask you . . . do you drink?" "Oh no Mum, I don't. Occasionally, I might have a guiness, but never whiskey."

Then she asked me if she would be expected to wash Jamie's clothes. "Only the Banlons," I said. I told her that she would get Wednesdays and Sundays off, and asked her if that was alright. She paled, and said, "Sundays is fine, Mum, but Wednesdays, all me friends are off on Thursday." "Well, never mind, take Thursdays off." I asked her if she wanted to see her room and called Hazel to "show" it. The room the girl saw aint hardly no maid's room. It was a huge bedroom with plenty light, double bed, telephone, T.V., bathroom, lots of closet space . . . The poor girl took a look and her eyes lit up and she exclaimed, "Ah, is this to be me room?"

Hazel and I looked at each other, and for a fleeting moment, I felt bad, but then I remembered that it wasn't my bedroom either. I slept on a fold-up couch, which wasn't hardly no Castro Convertible, so I continued.

The girl asked if she could have visitors. I said, "Of course you may. Just let me know a week in advance." We went back to the dining room and discussed salary. I asked her what she expected to get, and she said, "Same as on the card from the agency, $100.00 a week to start." Then she asked me what time Jamie went to bed. "7:30 P.M." "Oh, then after 8:00 P.M. I'm free, right?" "Right on!" I asked her if there were any other questions and she said, "No mum, I'm finished." I said, "So am I." I told her that I would speak to my husband and call the agency and they'd let her know. Now on the card from the agency "serving New York's most distinguished families," it stated that the carfare was to be paid by the employer. I handed the girl two tokens and she recoiled, shook her head and said, "Oh, no!" I said: "Please don't be silly, it's done all the time." She all but yelled—"No mum, I can't take it." I thought to myself, aint this a bitch. She can't take nothing from me. No coffee. No carfare. But she could take the $100.00 a week.

I called Hazel to fetch her coat and show her out. As she left the room I put out my hand to shake with her. Hers was wet and limp. She said, "I'm sorry that I wore pants and a sweater, mum." "Oh, that's all right, it's not a uniform job. Wear what you please, long as it's clean." I turned and walked away as she went out the door. I heard Hazel say to her, "Good luck."

Of course, I never called the agency. Although the "girl" told me she was interested, I'm sure when she went back to her sisters and told them of the Black Mrs. B., they'd send her back to Ireland before they'd let her take the job.

Hazel told me stories about her life in service. One about a woman whom Hazel said was a real mother. She did everything according to Dr. Spock (the old edition). Everything for her baby was planned and clinically clean, scientifically calculated. Hazel said that the woman would give her a chart when she came in to work each day, so that she could fill in the time she changed the diaper, gave bottles, etc. Everything was detailed and well planned for the baby. Hazel didn't find that too far out, but she did find it strange that at night the woman would place a carton of pacifiers in the baby's crib. The baby would search for a pacifier, fall asleep and all through the night keep changing pacifiers. Hazel said come morning the mother would take the broom, sweep all the pacifiers up and put them back in the carton. Hazel said once she asked her why she didn't wash them and the mother said, "because he'd think they were new."

Hazel mentioned the fact that many times the employer arranged her schedule so that the Black help ate meals separately from the white help and of course separately from the family. Said Hazel: "One time the people I worked for were eating dinner and they were talking about 'the girl' they had before and how terribly unappreciative, etc., she had been." The man said, "Hazel, you do appreciate all we do for you don't you? All the clothes Missus gives you and I know you appreciate the fact that we let you eat at the table with us." Hazel said, "did you ever notice that I don't eat nothing, that I only drink water from the kitchen, too. I don't enjoy sitting down at your table looking at the hair on your chest and seeing your underwears. You might be sexy for your wife but not for me. I don't enjoy watching you grab the food, slobber at the mouth and stick your fingers in everything. At my house, we eat with manners and more than that, my dining room set is better than yours and finally, I don't enjoy eating with crackers anyhow."

Hazel told me a lot about the Domestic Business on Park Avenue. All the class and caste systems among the Carriage Set. Hazel said in the park it is more a question of class than color. A nanny of a upper middle class baby is higher up than the nursemaid of a rich one. A plain old maid of either rich or upper middle class employers is lower than a mother's helper.

She said the snobbishness goes so deep that if your rank aint the same rank as theirs, they don't let you near the carriage.

Sometime they won't let you look in the carriage. "Don't go near the carriage," they will say, "the mother is funny." But it's a lie . . . says Hazel . . . it's them!

"Once in the park, they asked me if I was a governess or a maid. I said, 'Neither. I am a R.N.' 'A registered nurse! If you are, where is you cap and you pin? Why don't you wear it?' Can you imagine asking me how come I wasn't WALKING around wearing my cap and my pin? So I say to them: 'Listen, I don't show, *I* produce.'

"I always let everybody come near my carriage or stroller. You take the last little boy I took care of. He was the ugliest thing you ever saw. But he had more hugs and kisses than anybody. I let everybody play with him. It was better for me. The child grew up to be friendly and didn't stay right up under me and I could read if I wanted to."

Inside a house, with interracial help, much more snobbishness goes on than in the Park. Again, according to Hazel, "The white servants act like the Black servants don't know anything." Once, I was working for a lady with a young baby and in the presence of the white housekeeper, I said: "It's getting cooler, you'll need a bunting for the baby." The white housekeeper shouted: "bunting, what's bunting? I never heard of such a thing. Where did you ever hear the word?" The lady of the house laughed and said, "Hazel, did you make that up, ha, ha?" I was so mad, I tell you, so I said, "listen my dears, bunting have been in existence for many years. We were civilized where I come from and everybody know to say the word bunting. Maybe where you from, they don't ever wrap up the baby, huh?"

"But it's always like that, the white servants are always putting down the authority of the Black ones. They like to give the appearance that we don't know nothing."

A servant is someone who quits with little or no notice.

"You've got a lot of nerve quitting after all I've done for you. I gave you all our outgrown clothing; I could have given them to the Good Will people. That old suit I gave your boy, I could have put in the Men's Exchange on concession. Gave you our 17 inch T.V., all you had to do was to get it fixed. Let you have anything in the refrigerator to eat, sold you our old car for $250 when we could have gotten $300 from a dealer, let you have Broadway tickets at '2 for' rates when we could have sold them to scalpers for 4 times as much, let you have days off to go down South everytime one of your goddamned cousins died, loaned you the money for the fare—with no interest either—and you've got the nerve to serve me with 2 weeks' notice! I've got to go to Palm Beach on Saturday. I don't have time to look for another nigger to replace you. Hell, you can't do that to me. I'll call your landlord, I'll have you evicted, I'll cut off your credit at the corner store, and you will see the devil before you ever see another job in Westchester County, I'll see to that."

A servant used to be someone you could talk to anyway you wanted.

A servant was a young Black girl who slept in as a mother's helper for $1 a day in Mobile, Alabama, and if you wanted to take in a show at night, would take care of your kids for you and if the Joneses and the Smiths wanted to go would take care of their kids too.

A servant is like one of the family.

Onliest person I ever knew who was truly treated like one of the family, was my friend Lilly Mae, and her mother.

Lilly Mae's experience is unique, to say the least. Lilly Mae's mother worked for the Stanfords over 20 years. Lilly Mae grew up in the lap of luxury. The Stanfords consisted of an elderly childless couple who had old money. They must have had a bunch, cause Lilly Mae remembers that the help had help.

The Stanfords were more Yankees than Wasps. They were people of unusual character and genuine "goodness."

The Stanfords, Lilly Mae and her mother, Mahalia, lived in a three story town house on Beacon Street in the Back Bay area of Boston. Mahalia and Lilly Mae had the ground floor.

> "Mother called it the cellar. We had two bedrooms, a sitting room and a bath. The top floor was rented. It was a huge house. There was an elevator, too. There was an apartment over the garage where the chauffeur lived. Later, the chauffeur got married and came in by the day."

Lilly Mae and Mahalia (who was the housekeeper) were the only Black members of the Stanford's staff which consisted of a butler, carpenter, Irish laundress, four major maids and two minor maids (to help the majors). The chauffeur drove the Stanford's Packard and Cadillac.

> "I was born in the house on Beacon Street. Mother was supposed to go to the hospital, but I came first. My godmother, who was a registered nurse, was with mother and she delivered me. Daddy was away at sea most of the time. He was in the navy."

At this point, let me describe Lilly Mae. She is Black as the earth in Orange County, New York, which is black as coal. Lilly Mae is now in her early forties, and her ebony face shines with a radiance of one who has beauty and sunshine within. Her face is crowned by a salt and pepper fro.

"The Stanfords provided a white nannie for me, since Mother was busy running the house. Mother used to tell the story of Nannie in her uniform pushing the carriage on the Esplanade of Back Bay, and a wealthy woman saw the fabulous coach carriage, uniformed nurse, and stopped to admire the baby. When she looked in, saw me, she screamed, 'Oh my goodness!' "

Another unusual circumstance, was that Mahalia had Fridays off.

"Mother was free in the evenings and we'd spend evenings in 'our' apartment. Every Friday night, we'd have dinner at the Chinese restaurant."

Lilly Mae was a spirited child around the town house, and had access to all of it. Her exploits make Eloise seem like a girl scout.

"Once, when Mama was closing the city house, and we were on our way to the country place in Marshfield, Massachusetts, Mama was double checking everything, and left me waiting with the white chauffeur, who put me down and went to talk to the upstairs maid next door. I spied the dutch cleanser, and proceded to 'help' Mother. Oh, it was awful. I smeared everything I could get at. Mother cried.

"Another time, the family was entertaining a senator for dinner. Usually, I ate with them, but since it was a special occasion, Mother called me earlier. Well, the afternoon of this particular evening, I'd been in the white maid's room and put on nail polish, lipstick, rouge, pancake—all the make-up I could find. Well, when Mother who was busy making the senator's dinner saw me, she shed a few more tears.

"We'd go part of the summer, to North Scituate, a typical wealthy Cape town. Everyone had their summer servants. We were on the beach, and Mother was talking to the butler, and I saw some summer servants. I said very excitedly to Mother, 'Here comes that Black man.' I thought Blackman was his name. Again, Mother cried.

"Oh yes, there was the time when we had a program at school and I had on a white dress, white socks, white ribbons, my hair was loose. I was dressed to the nines! It was a lovely spring day. As I was strolling along, day dreaming, a block away from school,

I came upon a truck that was making a coal delivery. The delivery men were out to lunch. The coal hole looked filled. I wasn't convinced, so I decided to test it. I fell in, white dress, ribbons, white socks and all. Nothing to do but crawl out and go home to Mama. Mama wept."

School for Lilly Mae was the local public school in the Back Bay area. The school was 99% white. Not a few of the white children were children of the servants.

"I was taken to school by the chauffeur: at school I didn't know I was different. My first realization came in the 3rd grade. The teacher always had trouble in the coat room. There was always a big space around my coat. The teacher told this one child to hang up her coat on the hook next to mine. The child was a buck teeth, red hair midget, whose father was a maitre'd at the Statler Hotel. Well, when the teacher told her that, she screamed, 'No, my nursemaid told me that black people have diseases and not to have anything to do with them.' When I got home and told Mama, she told Mrs. Stanford, who called the mother of the midget, and the nursemaid was fired."

The Stanfords treated Lilly Mae as a grandchild.

"Although they were childless, there were lots of children (nieces and nephews) who'd come to visit. Especially Thanksgiving. Thanksgiving was a ritual. It would always be the same. We'd get up early. Mother cooked. She was a fabulous cook. Their whole family came.

"We'd go see Santa Land. Santa came by airplane on the Esplanade. Back home after the parade and have a snack. I always had a new outfit, too. Then, we'd eat a huge dinner with the family. After dinner, Mr. Stanford would take all the children to the movies. After the movies, Mr. Stanford would show home movies taken at Thanksgiving. About 6:00 P.M., we'd have a cold supper, coffee, tea, cakes, pies, etc. To this day Thanksgiving is my favorite day."

I asked Lilly Mae if she thought every experience in the Stanford's house was positive or negative.

"Mother realized that it was not a realistic world, not a natural circumstance. When I was around eight, she and daddy rented a four room apartment, because she wanted me to have a home, and it was better. The year went on, and then one day Aunt Beth died. Aunt Beth was Mother's best friend. Aunt Beth had worked for years and years for an elderly woman, and when the woman died, she left Aunt Beth a lot of money, the house, all the furniture in it and the dog, a Boston Bull. This was on a Tuesday. On Thursday, Aunt Beth went into the hospital for a check-up, and died on Saturday. Mother said, 'That's it. It's time for a different life.' And that's what we had. Mother stayed with Mrs. Stanford long enough to train someone else. Mother was replaced by a white housekeeper. As a matter of fact, the Stanfords never had any more Black help.

"Mother took up nursing, and I went to art school. We went back every Thanksgiving to visit. They both are dead now. So is my mother. Sometimes, I see members of the family. Our relationship is still warm and friendly. In my early 20's, it bothered me to have had such an upbringing. Now, it doesn't bother me at all."

A servant is a Black girl arriving in New York City at the Port Authority Bus Terminal with her cardboard suitcase and going directly to the Employment Agency; in answer to an Ad in a Southern paper.

At the agency, she will wait for a prospective employer to hire her. If the employer doing the hiring is a male and she is pretty, she might get hired that day and not have to owe the Agency the "fee" for overnight at the YWCA or a cheap hotel.

A servant is the Black that the Census Bureau counts, when they go in those neighborhoods where you know aint no colored people and the Bureau answers back . . . Yes there is one.

A servant that couldn't get reservations on the *Titanic* because of prejudice . . . is lucky.

A servant can get more money, if they go to one of those "Domestic Training Schools" that teach you how to clean toilets faster and better.

When we came here and were instantly put to work, nobody asked us if we had taken a course in home economics or agriculture, child care, geriatrics, etc., but the times they are a changing.

A friend of mine told me that he went to a office building to get a job as a janitor and the dude asked him, "What method of toilet cleaning do you use."

I believe the servant problem is the reason we got so many dishwashers and frozen foods today. It happened that one day Oriel got uppity and said, "Miss Anne, if you think that I am gonna cook your food, iron your clothes, clean your house, take care of your kids, and give your husband some, all for $15.00 a week, you can suck my nose til my head cave in." Miss Anne then became upset. When Mr. Charlie came home she said, "Charles, I have fired Oriel, and if you think I am going to stand over a miniature furnace all day and breathe the foul odor of broiling flesh and stinking plants, and if you think that I will put my lilly white hands among the grease and slime of dirty dishes, you can sleep in the guest room tonight." Now, Mr. Charlie got real nervous (you know how W.F.'s are about their women), so he invented a dishwasher, and froze *everything*.

A servant is the high school girl in Phoenix, Arizona, Indian School, who gets "bused into town" each Saturday morning to work for subsistence wages in private homes.

A servant is the porter in a white barber shop that won't cut Black folks hair, but will pay him to sweep up the hairs, long as they aint nappy.

A servant is lazy.

I worked around these parts serving white folks all my life. If there is other jobs besides serving white folks then they is unbeknownst to me. My mama and daddy worked for the same white family that I'm working for now. Course, these days, I don't do so much since I'm old, but I does what I kin around the place and they pays me what they kin. The old man is dead and he was fair and square. But his son the one what I'm working for now, is an ornery cracker. Always yelling about dumb lazy niggers. He don't know them niggers ain't lazy. They just don't wanna work for him. My daddy used to say, "I guess niggers is lazy, in slavery, they worked all their lives for white folks who didn't do nothing! So when freedom come, niggers thought they could be free like the white folks, and do nothing, but sit on their asses all day."

Brother Oregon Territory
Charleston, S.C.
Born 1889

Now this thing about us being lazy. We "lazy" cause we get tired. Don't feel like always working for somebody else. How it feel, to work in a nice house, with dishwasher, vacuum cleaner, plenty closets, clean straight walls, a spotless, roachless kitchen, a tidy tile bathroom, toilets that always flush, and pink bathtubs, etc.—and then come home and hang your coat on a nail on the back of the door, to cook in a kitchen full roaches, look at paint peeled walls, go sit in a cruddy bathroom where even if all the tiles are there, they are mismatched, hope the toilet will flush this time without having to go next door and borrow the plunger.

As a young child, I remember when friends wanted to come to my house and was ashamed cause we didn't have a living room suite (until mama bought Mrs. Krader's old one) and drapes like the girls who lived in "nice" houses. It hurt to have an icebox when frigidaires had been in style for a long time.

I was fascinated with refrigerators and vacuum cleaners. I couldn't imagine how my mother managed to operate Mrs. Krader's vacuum cleaner, since we didn't have one at home. Matter of fact, we didn't even have a carpet sweeper. Actually, we had no need for one, since we didn't have a carpet, we had linoleum with a Persian carpet pattern.

Another thing that gets to me still is wearing white folks' old clothes. I dig thrift stores, but every once in a while I got to back up to get a running start and buy something new. I remember when I was about 14, Mrs. Krader had given me an old suit that belonged to her daughter, Zelda, who wasn't much older than I was. She was maybe 16 or 17. Anyhow, one day I was strolling down Ridge Avenue with some of my friends in my new suit. I ran into Zelda and she said: "Gee, my suit looks good on you. Glad it could be of some service to you." Service, my ass. Think how I felt, styling in front of my friends with a new suit, and run into the young white lady who gave it to me.

My friends all laughed at me saying, "Ha, ha, you told us your mother bought it on Germantown Avenue. A white girl give it you, and you was too shame to tell it."

Until this day I aint too keen on taking or wearing second-handed clothes. I don't even like the song "Second-Hand Rose."

A servant is a "good-humored housekeeper" who fries chicken and produces other delicacies, and keeps the stereo playing "appropriate background music: the theme song from *Gone With the Wind*," while Lyndon B. Johnson's Press Secretary writes about the ranch.[16]

A servant is help, and help is sometimes the maid, who often is the waitress, baby sitter, answering service, cook, chauffeur, psychiatrist, and laundress.

One should never let the help know the financial position of the family otherwise help might think you can afford to pay them more. In fact, it is a good idea to borrow money from the help every once in a while.

> "She asked me to loan her $10.00 because she was short on cash. I told her I couldn't go it, because she still owed me $5.00 from last time she was short."

It is also a good idea not to spoil help by giving them Christmas or birthday presents or bonuses. The traditional thing is to say or indicate that you will leave them something after you are gone (dead).

> "The Indians was right about the white man. He do talk with a forked tongue. My aunt worked for an old white couple for fourteen dollars a week. They kept saying that they had no 'capital' but when they died she would be adequately taken care of. Both of them were old and sickly. My aunt was the nurse, cook and housekeeper for them. They would tell her every other day, she would be rewarded when they were gone. My aunt kept on working, and each day she thought would surely be their last. Don't you know that it took them 10 years to die, and all that they left her was the bed pan to clean."

Even if you have come right out and told help that you are going to leave them something, more than likely nobody will believe them, your family will see that they don't get a thing, or the court will take care of it.

> "I had a cousin who worked for years (as long as I can remember she was working as a housekeeper for this man) in Newport, Rhode Island. He was a wealthy widower. He had no children,

[16] Liz Carpenter, *Ruffles and Flourishes*, p. x.

and little if any family—at least they never came around. When he died, he left my cousin the house. The 'family' (some distant cousins) appeared and said that he must not have been of sound mind, and that the housekeeper had exercised undue influence over him. She lost the house."

Good help is hard to find. Help just aint what it used to be. In the old days when the El Morocco was THE El Morocco, when Del Monico steaks were steaks and Murray Hill was THE place to live, and Harlem was THE place to party, one could get real help. One could go to the Bronx to the domestic slave market.

"The heaviest traffic is at 167th Street and Jerome Avenue where, on benches surrounding a green square, the victims wait grateful at least for some place to sit. At Simpson Street and Westchester Avenue they pose wearily against buildings and lampposts or scuttle about in an attempt to retrieve discarded boxes upon which to sit. Not only is human labor bartered and sold for the slave wage but human love is also a marketable commodity. Whether it is labor or love, the women arrive as early as eight a.m. and remain as late as one p.m. or until they are hired. In rain or shine, hot or cold, they wait to work for ten, fifteen, and twenty cents per hour. They wash floors, clothes, windows and etc."[17]

In the good old days one could advertise for exactly the kind of help one wanted. "Light colored help wanted. No dark need apply."
Nowadays, one has to beat around the bush. If one wants colored help (of any complexion) one has to say domestic. If one wants white, one has to say "European preferred." But there are still some sections of the country where one can get it on. Like out West, where what you advertise for is what you get.

Indian girl wanted to take care of house and to assist mother with 4 adorable bright children. Sleep in, own room, TV and $40.00 per week. Must be reliable, cheerful, have recent checkable references and must love children. Only non-drinkers need apply.

[17] Ottley and Weatherby, eds., *The Negro in New York*, pp. 269–70.

Used to be a servant was someone you could count on now, and pay later. But these are trying times. Everything's changing up. Nassau's gone funky. Tiny Tim's got a baby. Cash is almost obsolete. (There was a whole planeload of people getting their tickets when I went to Michigan recently, and I was the only one who used cash.) Flip Wilson is Geraldine. Poets poet different. And servants don't servant the same.

These days servants want a union, social security, health and accident insurance, respect, and weekends off.

IX

The Servants
Done Riz!

Household Workers Conference

The Professional Household Workers Local #1, a new and much needed union is affiliated with the International Brotherhood of Sleeping Car Porters. This seems like a most logical affiliation. For the Household Workers Union is composed largely of a Black membership. And, having come through the struggle for recognition many years ago, who better than the Sleeping Car Porters, also mainly Black, knows of the racial prejudices, the servile conditions, the ridiculous wages and a host of other ills that domestics are working under.

On April 8th, an all-day conference in behalf of household workers was held to (1) publicize and dramatize their exploitation which includes: low wages, long hours, and no paid holidays or vacations (2) to discuss the necessity for including them in the minimum wage law which will automatically give them the benefit of Workmen's Compensation, life insurance, fringe benefits, etc. (3) and most urgent, to highlight the need for them to become involved in the mainstream of the professional world of work.

The conference which was sponsored by the New York City Commission on Human Rights was chaired by Commissioner Eleanor Holmes Norton. Luncheon speakers were William Bowe, Secretary for the Central Labor Council, who represented Harry Van Arsdale and Elizabeth Duncan Koontz, Director of the U. S. Department of Labor Women's Bureau. Mrs. Koontz stated that the time has come to respect household workers as persons providing a service: the day of payment "in kind" for services rendered is over.[1]

A housewife in Great Neck called her husband at his office and said hysterically, "Charles, help. Help. I need some help! Charles, Jr., is somewhere in the East Village. Little Sally has joined the Hari

[1] *Breakthrough*, Vol. 2, No. 2.

Krishna! And Beulah's done gone and joined the Maids' Lib! I don't know what I'm going to do. Listen to this note Beulah left me!"

Dear Ms. Anne:
By the time you get home from your Womens' Lib meeting, I will be gone. Your house is just as you and your untidy family left it. I only came in this morning to pick up my belongings, my sweaters, my galoshes and my silver tray that I loaned you for that Sisterhood meeting you had recently. You can keep the uniform, but please send me the $5.00 I gave you for taxi fare when you were short.

Knowing and appreciating how much yall depended on me, I sure hated to leave like this without notice. But then, I remembered that summer before last when you couldn't cope and went to Europe for two months. You never gave me no notice. And last year, when you and Mr. Charles had a fight and he moved into a hotel and you went to your mother's, I was out of work for two weeks with no notice or pay. And after yall made up and went to Bermuda for a second honeymoon, yall didn't give me no notice and no pay. Oh, I want to tell you, remember that time when I told you I was on jury duty? It was a lie. I had my appendix out, but I knew you wouldn't pay me for that, so I said jury duty, because Mr. Charles is a corporation lawyer and I know he would not mess with the government. I came back to work two weeks early, cause I couldn't afford to stay off no longer. Plenty days I worked when I was sick and needed to be in bed, but I needed the money, so I had to work. Plenty of days I had "female trouble" same as you. Did it ever occur to you that I gets cramps too? So, when I think of how unfair you might feel I am to leave you with no notice, I remember all the times you have caused hardships to me and I don't feel bad. I feel bad that I didn't do it sooner.

I know that it is going to be hard on you, adjusting your schedule, etc., but it can be done. Don't forget that after I left your house, I went home to raise four children. And speaking of my children, you know all those clothes you gave them? Well they never did wear them. They didn't think they were fly or "bad" enough. Thank God for my children. It is through them that I have become enlightened. Last night they took me to a meeting that was held at our church. It was a meeting of the maids. We all testified. After we told our stories, we decided to come together as a group. We formed the U.M.L.F. The United Maids Liberation Front. I am the chairman of the Board. Our headquarters are at 126th Street and Lenox Avenue. Come up and see me sometime.

Here are a few suggestions I can give you to help you get by: When you wax the floor, be sure to completely remove all the old wax before adding the new. Use clean, dust free rags when you wash the windows, and don't use steel wool on the stainless steel pots. It scratches.

I would suggest you schedule your bra burning demonstrations in the latter part of the afternoon. That will give you time to clean, shop and finish most of your pre-dinner preparations.

Please don't feel that all is over. I or someone like me would be most willing to work for you under the following conditions as worked out by our steering committee. A written work contract that would include (this is a partial list):

1. Paid vacations and sick leave. Legal holidays with pay.
2. Establish an employer-employee relationship
3. Explain exactly what you want done (define what the job is)
4. A minimum of two dollars an hour
5. Double time for overtime
6. Time and form of payment (Cash or check. Most of us don't have checking accounts no how, and the over-priced corner grocery stores usually don't cash no checks anyway.)
7. R.E.S.P.E.C.T.

From this list you get an idea of the working conditions that would lure me back to work for you.

Please feel free to call me if you run into any problems round the house. We have a "girl" who advises former employers. Just call and ask for extension HELP.

> Sincerely yours,
> Aisha
> (slave name, Beulah)

BIBLIOGRAPHY

Angelou, Maya. *Just Give Me a Cool Drink of Water 'For I Die*. New York: Random House, 1971.

Aptheker, Herbert. *American Negro Slave Revolts*. New York: International Publishers, 1943.

Bennett, Lerone. *Before the Mayflower: A History of the Negro in America, 1619–1964*. New York: Penguin, 1964.

Botkin, Benjamin A. *Lay My Burden Down: A Folk History of Slavery*. Chicago: University of Chicago Press, 1945.

Carpenter, Liz. *Ruffles and Flourishes*. Garden City: Doubleday, 1970.

Carroll, Joseph C. *Slave Insurrections in the United States, 1800–1865*. Westport: Negro Universities Press, 1938.

Chapman, Abraham, ed. *Black Voices: An Anthology of Afro-American Literature*. New York: New American Library, 1968.

Childress, Alice. *Like One of the Family*. New York: Knopf, 1967.

Cullen, Countee. *On These I Stand*. New York: Harper & Row, 1969.

Du Bois, W. E. B. *The Gift of Black Folk: The Negroes in the Making of America*. Chicago: Johnson Reprint, 1969.

Evans, Mari. *I Am a Black Woman*. New York: Morrow, 1971.

Freyre, Gilberto. *The Masters and the Slaves*. New York: Knopf, 1964.

Hughes, Langston. *Ask Your Mama*. New York: Knopf, 1961.

——. *Simple's Uncle Sam*. New York: Hill & Wang, 1965.

Ingraham, J. H. *The Sunny South: Or, the Southerner at Home*. Atlanta: Negro University Press, 1860.

Jones, LeRoi and Neal, Roy, eds., *Black Fire*. New York: Morrow, 1968.

Lee, Don L. *Don't Cry, Scream*. Detroit: Broadside Press Publications, 1969.

Mannix, Daniel B., and Cowley, Malcolm. *Black Cargoes: A History of the Atlantic Slave Trade, 1518–1865*. New York: Viking Press, 1962.

Osofsky, Gilbert, ed. *Puttin on Ole Massa: The Slave Narratives of Henry Bibb, William W. Brown, and Solomon Northrup*. New York: Harper & Row, 1969.

Ottley, Roi, and Weatherby, William J., eds. *The Negro in New York: An Informal Social History 1626–1940*. New York: Praeger, 1969.

Oyono, Ferdinand. *Houseboy*. New York: Collier Books, 1970.

Rogers, J. A. *Sex and Race*. Privately published: New York, 1944.

Shaw, Maud. *White House Nanny*. London: Frewin, 1968.

Shoener, Allen, ed. *Harlem on My Mind 1900–1918*. New York: Knopf, 1964.

Social Science Institute, Fisk University. *Unwritten History of Slavery*. Washington: NCR Microcard Editions, 1968.

Spero, S. D., and Harris, A. L. *The Black Worker: The Negro and the Labor Movement*. New York: Atheneum, 1969.

Stampp, Kenneth M. and Litwack, Leon F., eds. *Reconstruction: An Anthology of Revisionist Writings*. Baton Rouge: Louisiana State University Press, 1969.

Still, William. *The Underground Railroad*. Chicago: Johnson Publishing Company, 1970.

Sydnor, Charles S. *Slavery in Mississippi*. Baton Rouge: Louisiana State University Press, 1966.

Tindall, George Brown. *South Carolina Negroes, 1877–1900*. Baton Rouge: Louisiana State University Press, 1966.

Vogue magazine. *The World of Vogue*. New York: Viking Press, 1963.

Wesley, Charles H., and Romero, Patricia W. *Negro Americans in the Civil War—From Slavery to Citizenship*. Washington: United Publishing Corporation, 1967.

Wyley, Bell Irvin. *The Life of Billy Yank*. Garden City: Doubleday, 1971.

PERMISSIONS

Vertamae Smart-Grosvenor (1937–2016) was an American culinary anthropologist, griot, food writer, and broadcaster on public media. She wrote several books on African American cooking, including *Vibration Cooking: or, The Travel Notes of a Geechee Girl*, an autobiographical cookbook and memoir.

Premilla Nadasen is professor of history at Barnard College, Columbia University. She is author of several books, including *Household Workers Unite: The Untold Story of African American Women Who Built a Movement*.